Dickie Bird is the most [...] ation. He has stood in [...] including 67 Test mat[...] He also played First [...] Leicestershire. His enormous contribution to cricket was recognised in July 1996 when he was awarded the MBE. He has umpired in four World Cup tournaments, and stood in the finals of the first three, as well as in the women's World Cup in 1982, including the final. He has umpired all the major domestic cup finals, the Gillette, NatWest and Benson & Hedges; and all over the world, including the Asia Cup and Rothman's Cup in Sharjah. He won a People of the Year Award in 1996, and has written a number of bestselling books. An honorary life member of the MCC, Yorkshire CC and Leicestershire CC, he retired from the First Class List in 1998 and lives in Barnsley.

Dickie Bird

Not Out

ORION

An Orion paperback

First published in Great Britain by Arthur Barker Limited in 1978
This paperback edition published in 1999 by Orion Books Ltd,
Orion House, 5 Upper St Martin's Lane, London WC2H 9EA

A CIP catalogue record for this book is available from the
British Library.

ISBN: 0 75282 763 4

Printed and bound in Great Britain by
Clays Ltd, St Ives plc

Contents

List of Illustrations

Acknowledgements

Many good people have helped me with this book and I would like to thank them all, most sincerely. First, Donald Carr, secretary of the Test and County Cricket Board, for giving me permission to go ahead with it while I am still an active umpire.

I owe a large debt to my many friends in the local Press, to the staff at the *Barnsley Chronicle*, and to all those who have assisted me at the *Sheffield Star*, *Sheffield Morning Telegraph*, *Yorkshire Post* and *Coal News*.

The photographs have come from a variety of sources and I thank especially Roy Sabine of Barnsley and the award-winning sports photographer Eric Piper of the London *Daily Mirror*. I am very appreciative of the fact that the Rt. Hon. Roy Mason took time off from his awesome duties as Secretary of State for Northern Ireland to pose for pictures.

Finally, a special thank you to my friend Brian Scovell of the *Daily Mail* for his journalistic help and kindness, and a blanket thank you to the many people who helped me with my cricket career.

DICKIE BIRD
Barnsley, 1978

Not Out

I

The Nightmare Job

In the High Court action between Kerry Packer's company and the world cricketing authorities the former England fast bowler John Snow was asked about his future employment prospects when he finished playing. Would he like to become an umpire? 'The thought of that gives me nightmares,' he said.

I don't have nightmares though my mother, with whom I live in a bungalow called 'The Wickets' in Staincross, Barnsley, does say that often she hears me shouting in the night 'that's out!' or 'catch it, catch it'. Umpiring in Test matches is a considerable strain.

The players, who can now earn £1,000 for a single Test, stay in the best hotels whereas umpires stay at smaller places, usually within walking distance of the grounds. For five months in the summer it is a hard slog round the country, with little rest. I don't mind the physical strain so much, standing in the middle for six hours. But the mental strain can be taxing. Most nights I am so tired that after an evening meal I usually go straight to bed. I am not often up and about after 10.30.

For all that, I wouldn't do any other job. I think it is a wonderful life, the next best thing to playing the game. Cricket is full of humour and rich experiences and I am proud to be a part of it. It is an enjoyable life, and the satisfaction derived from it is worth more to me than any amount of money. If I wasn't happy, I would quit tomorrow. I started comparatively young, at the age of thirty-six, and I hope I am still standing (I mean as an umpire!) in 1999 when I shall be sixty-five and due to retire.

It does worry me slightly, though, that some of the best big-match umpires have not lived a long life. Arthur Fagg died in 1977 at the age of sixty-two and two of England's most respected umpires, Frank Chester and Sid Buller, died at sixty-one. Chester died of duodenal ulcers and Buller had a fatal heart attack while doing a game at Edgbaston in 1970.

All the first-class umpires, with the exception of Don Oslear, have played first-class cricket. I think this is why we are respected by the players: we know the game as well as they do. This is not the case in professional football, where few referees have played the game at a high level. Oslear, who played football professionally for Grimsby Town, Hull City and Oldham Athletic, makes up for his lack of playing experience with his knowledge of the laws of cricket. He will take a bet any time about a point of law – and he doesn't lose his money!

When I was playing cricket, I never thought about becoming an umpire. After I left Leicestershire, I became a coach in South Africa. In 1969 my father died and I came home for the funeral. It was a sad time because my father had been such a great influence on my life. He was a coal-miner from the age of thirteen and he retired at sixty-five. He had dust in the lungs and lived only five more years. He didn't see too much of life or the outside world. He'd never been abroad and most of his working life was stuck below the ground working at a coal seam. I went down the mine several times myself and it horrified me. Sometimes the seam would be just eighteen inches high. When he crawled through, his trousers would get caught and he'd carry on without them.

In those days miners had no automatic tools or conveyor belts to take away the coal. They had to hack it out with picks and throw it into the tubs. Then they had to push the tub back to the bottom of the shaft themselves, often a journey of two or more miles.

By the time my father came home from work early in the afternoon he would be so tired that after tea he would go to bed.

I revered him, but I decided at an early age that I would never follow him down the pit. He was a virtuous man and he put me right for life. Don't smoke, he used to say. And don't drink. And don't mess about with girls, either. Even now, I don't smoke cigarettes, only the occasional cigar, and I drink very little, just half a lager or a beer with the Australians in their dressing-room after a day's play (you can't refuse an Australian!).

I remain a bachelor although I must confess there were three occasions when I came close to marriage, though I was never engaged. Each time I backed out because I didn't think it would be fair to a girl to be married to someone who was rarely at home. My father never had much money, but there was always a joint on the table on Sundays and he stinted himself to buy me cricket equipment when I joined Barnsley Cricket Club as a fifteen-year-old. My parents taught me the proper values, about giving, and about respecting other people. My mother was a good woman who worked tirelessly on our behalf. About the only time she got out of the house was to take us to church on Sundays.

After my father's funeral I went to Headingley, where I used to be a Yorkshire player, to watch a day's play between York-shire and Derbyshire in the county championship. Some of my best friends were playing, Don Wilson and Doug Padgett, now coaches, among them. They asked me if I missed the first-class game. I said I did. One of them said, 'Why don't you become an umpire, that will keep you in touch?' I liked the idea and wrote to Donald Carr, secretary of the Test and County Cricket Board at Lord's. Soon afterwards, I had a letter back saying I had been accepted.

There was no examination to pass. I had already taken the laws of the game when I qualified as an Advanced MCC Coach. But first I had to undergo a stiff medical examination, with the emphasis on ears and eyes. Each season, umpires have to repeat their medical. Anyone whose eyesight or hearing is failing runs the risk of being removed from the list. I am a fitness fanatic myself. I train in the winters, running in South Africa, where until 1977 I coached, and doing exercises at home. Brian

Johnston, the radio commentator, always said I was the fastest umpire in the business and if there were an Olympic event for running backwards, I would be an obvious favourite. If there is a chance of a run out, it is essential that the umpire gets himself into the right position, level with the batting crease, as quickly as he can. I make a point of running to the side of the wicket where the ball has been played. All the action is in front of me then, and I can see if the wicket keeper or fielder takes the ball cleanly.

I make one exception to this rule: if the ball is played in the direction of extra cover. If it is, you stand a good chance of being struck by the fielder's return throw if you are standing that side of the wicket. I have been hit several times, but never hurt.

I was born on 19 April 1933 in a two-up, two-down terraced house in Church Lane in the centre of Barnsley. We had no bathroom – we had a tub we used to take down off the back of the door and fill up with water in front of the fire – and an outside toilet. The houses have since been pulled down and that bit of land is now a traffic island. Within two years we moved to a house on the New Lodge Estate, Smithies, which had an extra bedroom and a proper bathroom.

I was christened Harold (after my father, whose full name was James Harold) Dennis Bird but from an early age was called Dickie. I don't know how it first started. Kids use these names and they stick. I didn't like it, Dickie Bird sounded like a micky take, but I soon accepted it. Most of the kids on that estate had nicknames. One of my best friends was Tommy Taylor, later to become the Manchester United and England centre-forward; we called him 'Tucker'. I don't know whether that was because he used to tuck them away with his head – I always said he was as good as Tommy Lawton in the air – or whether it was something to do with his appetite.

We used to play football on a rough piece of ground every day until dark in the winter. Tommy used to say, 'Give it to me in the air.' I think that was because he couldn't afford boots and his old 'tackies', battered plimsolls, always had holes in them.

This made him brilliant in the air when he became a pro. These impromptu matches nearly always ended in fights.

In the summer, we would play cricket on the same pitch. It would have stones and broken glass strewn over it and the home-made ball would fly off at some alarming angles. Anyone who was frightened of being hit didn't play. You got used to the knocks and I think it was this early training which gave me the confidence to face up to fast bowlers like Frank Tyson, Fred Trueman and Brian Statham when I played county cricket. I may not have been a particularly good batsman, but I got behind the ball. I never lacked guts.

I played in the same school's soccer side as Tommy Taylor and I remember one day he was left out of the team by the master in charge, Arthur Hudson, because he didn't have football boots, only a pair of clogs. His was a tragic family. His father, like mine a coal-miner, went blind and his mother died of cancer. Tommy died in the Manchester United air crash at Munich in 1958. He was burned alive and there were only a few ashes left from his remains to put into the casket.

Another of my friends was Arthur Rowe, the Olympic shot putter. Arthur, Tommy and myself were inseparable. We used to walk to school together most mornings and play football and cricket in break times. Arthur ought to have won a medal in the 1960 Olympic Games in Rome, but as soon as he got his track suit off he lost all confidence. 'I just froze up, Dickie,' he told me afterwards. Later, he became a Rugby League player.

At fifteen I was set to do a Willie Watson or a Brian Close, play both football and cricket professionally. That was my ambition. Harold Rushworth, the sports master at Raley School, made me school captain although I was the smallest player in the side. The school had no cricket pitch but cricket was played on the flattest part of the soccer pitch. It wasn't a good wicket!

During the lunch intervals, Mr Rushworth and Mr Arthur Hudson, another teacher, used to get the boys to give them batting practice on the asphalt playground. Both teachers played for Wombwell at the time. They put pennies instead of bails on the stumps and if we knocked them off, we could have them. It was a useful way of earning sweet money.

Mr Rushworth recommended me to Barnsley Football Club, the local Football League club, and I went along there for training. Tommy Taylor and some of my friends were all there and 'Jock' Steele, the coach, used to work us hard. 'Jock' is still with the club as general manager. Few people in professional football have survived for so long at one club as he has: it is over thirty years now. Mr Rushworth is also still actively involved in Barnsley's sporting life.

I was playing for Barnsley Schools at both cricket and football and was an amateur with Barnsley FC. One day I was down to play for the Barnsley Northern Intermediate team at Hull but the pitch was waterlogged and the match was postponed. I played for Barnsley YMCA in a local youth league instead and damaged my knee. I needed a cartilage operation and never played football seriously again.

So it was cricket or nothing if I was going to become a successful sportsman. I took myself off to the Barnsley Cricket Club nets with my boots, shirt and trousers in a carrier bag and the first person I saw at the club, I asked, 'Can I have a trial?' The man looked at me disapprovingly and said, 'Run away.'

I could have been lost to the game. But another member, Alf Broadhead, a slow left-arm bowler and a railway worker, shouted after me, 'Here, what's your name? Come and bowl to me in the net.'

At the time I was a pace bowler but I could bat too. I was a right-hander without too many shots, a nudger and a pusher. Alf Broadhead was a tremendous encouragement to me and I owed him a lot for helping me to develop into a county cricketer. There were some distinguished fellow players in the Barnsley club in those years.

One of them was Michael Parkinson, the TV personality and writer. I opened the batting with him many times. We called him Mick, or sometimes 'Parky'. He was a pretty useful left-hand batsman, full of confidence but perhaps lacking in shots. He wasn't county class, although he always said that was his big ambition, to open the batting for Yorkshire. He went to the Yorkshire nets once and wasn't invited back. But he was a good League cricketer, well worth his place. At the time, he was a reporter on the *South Yorkshire Times*.

I remember once playing in a match with him at the Shaw Lane Ground and it was one of those days when the pitch needed patting down a lot. I used to give it a right whack. You could hear it right round the ground. A wag shouted out, 'Here, don't hit it too hard, Birdie, there's men working under there.' He was right. The Dodworth Colliery runs under the ground!

Later, after I had become the £4 a week professional at Barnsley, we had another confident young lad turning up from Fitzwilliam, a mining village about seven miles from my home. His name was Geoffrey Boycott and, like me, he was the son of a miner. I'd never known anyone so dedicated to getting to the top. Even in those days he knew where he was going.

In later years, he would rib me by greeting me, 'Hello Richard, how are you?' It is a big joke in the Yorkshire dressing-room. He is the only person who calls me Richard and he knows it needles me. Boycott's nickname in his younger days was 'Fiery'. I think he got it because of the way he used to throw his bat down after getting out. He hated being dismissed. Nowadays, fewer people call him 'Fiery'. He's 'Boyks' or simply Geoffrey (in Yorkshire) or Geoff (around the rest of the country).

When I left school at fifteen, I started a job at the pit as a fitter. There weren't many other places you could find work in Barnsley except at a coal-mine. But I wasn't going to go underground. Not even for £135 a week! Being employed by the National Coal Board saved me from having to go on National Service.

Barnsley CC recommended me to Yorkshire County Cricket Club for a trial, but it wasn't easy to get the time off in midweek. I asked the pit manager, Edward Charlton, known as 'Chunky', if I could have a day off, and he said, 'No, and if you take it, I'll sack thee.'

He was a very astute fellow. He knew that I was looked on

locally as a useful all-rounder so he did a deal: a day off if I would agree to playing in the pit knock-out competition which I was not eligible to play in because I was a pro with Barnsley. I played under an assumed name, George Copping. The other players knew who I was and objected but 'Chunky' over-ruled them all and we won.

'Chunky' was an incredible character and though he has long since retired to the North East, the miners still talk about him in the pubs in Barnsley. In another knock-out competition for miners, he played a fellow named Harry Beachey who was ineligible. Harry wasn't needed really because we made a big score and won easily. Afterwards, the organizing committee called 'Chunky' in to see them to tell him that they were awarding the cup to the losing side because his team had broken the rules.

Four members of the committee worked under 'Chunky' at the colliery. 'Don't come in for work tomorrow,' he said. 'You're sacked.' Cricket meant a lot to him! Eventually it was sorted out with 'Chunky' getting his way again.

One day I was at the colliery when he came in to the fitting shop demanding to see the engine wright. I said I didn't know where he was. 'Is he in his office over there?' asked 'Chunky'. He tried the door. The engine wright, Jack Schofield, had locked himself in. Like a few others, he was scared of Mr Charlton. 'Chunky' seized a big hammer and literally smashed the door down. Things have changed a bit in coal-mining since then!

It was a nerve-wracking bus journey to Headingley for my first appearance in the Yorkshire nets. To a Yorkshire lad, the thought of playing alongside great cricketers like Len Hutton, Johnny Wardle and Bob Appleyard was like a Catholic being summoned to the Vatican to meet the Pope. Brian Clough, the football manager, has often said he would give up everything in football just for one game of cricket in the Yorkshire side. There is a mystique about Yorkshire cricket which only people born in the county can understand.

I had my own bat with me, a Sugg, and it was covered with

lashings of oil. As I walked into the gates at Headingley, I was a bag of nerves. The chief coach, Arthur Mitchell, met me. 'Well lad,' he said. 'What does tha do?'

'I'm a batsman, Mr Mitchell,' I said. He pointed to a net and said, 'Put thee pads on and git in there.' The bowlers in that particular net were Bob Appleyard, one of the finest exponents of the off cutter in the game, Johnny Wardle, the slow left-arm bowler who took 1,846 wickets between 1946 and 1968 and was then at his peak, and an eighteen-year-old fast bowler named Fred Trueman. To make it worse, the pitch was rain-affected. Wardle bowled the first ball to me. It turned and lifted and my forward prod was some inches away from it. Then Appleyard bowled and that one went through the gate. Trueman ran in and I was a bit late on it, failing to connect yet again.

I was in the net fifteen minutes and I can still recall every delivery. I failed to hit one. After my allotted time, Mitchell came over and said, 'If tha going to play like that, tha better not come back again.' He was like that, always highly critical and never much of a morale booster. They called him 'Ticker', a nickname he acquired on a tour of India when he was known as 'Ticker Sahib'. But you knew he was right most of the time and that he would make you a better player. I learned a lot from Maurice Leyland, the other coach. He taught me to keep perfectly still as the bowler went into his delivery stride. It is a good piece of advice and I often think about it as I watch some of the modern players picking their bats up and moving around – Tony Greig and Mike Brearley among them – before the bowler has bowled. Barry Richards doesn't move. And he's a great player. Most great players keep still.

It is a hard school in Yorkshire but I think it gives you the hungry fighter philosophy which takes many sportsmen to the peak of their profession. One of the locals in Barnsley at this time was Dorothy Hyman, the sprinter. She used to do her training running up and down the slagheaps. One night she was out running in the dark when she crashed her head into an iron bar. It didn't deter her from training at night afterwards.

I signed as a professional with Yorkshire in 1952 at £12.50 a week but, though I was quite successful in the second team, it wasn't until 1957 that I made my first-team début against Derbyshire at Headingley. Brian Stott, another left-hander, and I put on fifty for the first wicket. Opening the bowling for Derbyshire was a former miner, Les Jackson. He had a tremendous pair of shoulders and I always rated him as one of the best faster bowlers of his time. He was a killer bowler!

Language out in the middle can be pretty bad these days but it couldn't be worse than that used in the Yorkshire team in my early days. There were a lot of perfectionists in the side and none of them tolerated inefficiency. One day we were playing Surrey at Bradford and Johnny Wardle was bowling to Peter May. Johnny brought Mike Cowan into mid wicket and bowled a Chinaman. Peter May went for the drive and hit it straight at Cowan, who dropped it. Wardle's language was fearful. 'I'm ever so sorry, Johnny,' said Cowan. 'I didn't drop it on purpose.'

'Bugger off out to the boundary,' said Wardle, pointing to the fence. Next ball, Wardle bowled another Chinaman. May struck it up in the air again, a steepler towards Cowan. Wardle stood in the middle of the pitch, arms crossed. 'He'd better catch the bugger this time,' he said.

Cowan got under the ball but was so terrified at what might happen if he dropped it that he didn't get a hand to it. The ball bounced into his chest and away. Wardle was beside himself. At the end of the over, Cowan, tears in his eyes, came over to Wardle and said: 'I'm ever so sorry, Johnny.' Wardle looked at him and replied, 'Don't worry, lad. It were my fault for putting you there.' These cricketing gods did have a human side as well!

No-one on the staff was allowed to become big-headed. Don Wilson arrived for a trial and kept being bowled. He was a joiner making coffins in Settle at the time and when he came out at the net Arthur Mitchell said to him, 'Tha tells me tha's a joiner, lad. Well, when tha come tomorrow, bring thy tools and some boards and board that bloody end up when tha goes in to bat.'

The Yorkshire captain in my early years was Billy Sutcliffe.

I thought he was a fine player and if he had played for Middlesex, or some county other than Yorkshire, he would have been
acknowledged as a good cricketer. But in Yorkshire he was
always unfairly compared to his father, Herbert. He couldn't
win. The senior players gave him a difficult time.

He was succeeded as captain by Ronnie Burnett, a hard man
and in my opinion, a good captain. He led Yorkshire to the
championship, their first title since sharing first place with
Middlesex ten years earlier in 1959, and was then sacked. There
was an unhappy ending to the year for him, and me. In May,
Ken Taylor, the regular opening bat who was keeping me out of
the side, was selected to play for MCC against the Indians at
Lord's and I was called up for the Glamorgan match at
Bradford.

Glamorgan were bowled out for 137 in their first innings and
I played my highest and longest innings for Yorkshire – 181 not
out in 7¼ hours in Yorkshire's 405–8. My previous best score
up to then was 62. *Wisden* described me as a twenty-six-year-old
Colt (there have even been thirty-year-old Colts at Yorkshire)
who 'gave a great display of concentration'. They did mention,
however, that I was missed at 53 (on the boundary by Jim
Pressdee, a difficult one) and 102 (a straight forward lob to
Bernie Hedges at mid off which he said he didn't see).

When I got back to the dressing-room, Brian Sellers, the
chairman of selectors, was there to greet me. 'Well played,
Dickie lad,' he said. 'But get thee bloody head down, you're in
the second eleven in the next match.' That's Yorkshire cricket:
they deflate you before you can reflect in any glory. Sellers had
a lot of enemies but I liked him and respected him. He gave it
to you straight, never behind your back. That is another
admirable Yorkshire quality.

Yorkshire won the title at Hove at the end of August after
Robin Marlar, the Sussex captain, set them to score 215 in 105
minutes. It was a daft declaration really and no-one expected
us to do it, but Stott and Padgett made 141 in an hour, and we
won by five wickets.

I missed that game but was in the side that beat the MCC at

Scarborough in the next match. I don't know how we managed
to win that one because most of the players didn't arrive in
Scarborough until 4 a.m., after the champagne celebrations at
Hove, and when they got to the hotel, thousands of supporters
were waiting outside. The celebrations dragged on. It was quite
incredible that so many people should turn out in the middle of
the night.

I scored 58 and 0 against the MCC and fully expected to be
in the side for the final match against the Rest of England
at the Oval. When the names were read out, I wasn't in the
thirteen. It was a bitter blow. I'd always looked on myself as
a loyalist. I was proud to play for Yorkshire, but this was too
much. The other players had a whip round and paid my
expenses to attend the Oval.

I went to see Sellers and he said, 'Tha's got an argument
because tha's played well. But we've brought in Vic Wilson
because it's his farewell game. He's finishing.' He said I had a
future with the club and would definitely be playing the following season. I left a happier man. I'd sweat my blood to water
for Yorkshire.

One day in the winter, Ronnie Burnett rang me and appeared
to be very upset. 'What's up, skipper?' I said. 'You're crying.'

He said, 'I've got the sack.' I was amazed, more so when he
told me that Vic Wilson was his successor. It was felt at the time
that the committee wanted a younger man. Burnett was forty-
one. But Wilson, the new man, was thirty-nine and that season
he'd scored 359 runs in 15 matches for an average of 18.89
compared to Burnett's 366 runs, average 11.43. Anyway,
Wilson led Yorkshire to the championship in his first season
and scored 1,000 runs so perhaps the committee were right
after all, though it didn't seem so at the time.

In April, practice matches started and in one of the games I
scored 89 not out against the bowling of Trueman, Ray
Illingworth, Don Wilson and Brian Close. That was the day the
names of the thirteen players for the Southern tour were to be
announced. I was sitting next to Ted Lester, the present scorer,
who was second eleven captain at the time. 'I hope I won't see

you again this season,' he said. He wasn't being rude! He thought I ought to be a first-team regular. Sellers read the names out in alphabetical order. I wasn't in the Bs, perhaps he'd got it in lower down. But he hadn't. I wasn't in. I cried. I was twenty-six and I cried. I rushed out, got into the Ford Prefect I'd just bought for £400 and drove home.

My father was at home and he was just as distressed as I was. I said I was going to sit down and write for my release. He advised against it but I wrote all the same. It was the first time in my life I had failed to take his advice. I regret that I didn't, because leaving Yorkshire was the biggest mistake of my career. The Yorkshire Committee turned down my application the first and second times I wrote but gave in on the third. I was determined to leave. Sellers wrote saying he hoped I would remember my schooling in Yorkshire. I never forgot it.

Willie Watson, the former Yorkshire opener, was captain of Leicester at this time and asked me to come down to see him. I went the same day. Mike Turner, the new secretary of the club, was with him and impressed me. I signed immediately, almost without thinking. Leicester had finished 16th out of 17 in the championship and were a poor county with poor gates. I was on £500 a year and lived in digs in a pub, the Rutland and Derby Arms. The people who ran it were very nice but I couldn't sleep there. I had been a teetotaller but few teetotallers survive on the cricket circuit and I was drinking a few halves by then. I was never one for the late sessions though. I used to go to bed, but usually to toss and turn because I couldn't get to sleep for the noise.

I had a disastrous start to the season but picked up to make 1,000 runs by the end of it and was awarded my county cap. Watson was sacked and Maurice Hallam took over as captain. I never got on with Hallam. He seemed to dislike all Yorkshiremen. Leicester had a strong Yorkshire connection, for besides Watson and myself they also had Jack van Geloven, Peter Broughton and Bernie Cromack on the staff.

Hallam was an excellent batsman but he had a curious weakness for fast, short-pitched bowling. He was frightened of it,

though, paradoxically, he was a good hooker. He felt he should
have played for England and that Yorkshire players were stopping him. Worse players have been chosen for England and I
think he was rather unlucky not to get at least one cap.

In a match at Worcester I was racing round the boundary
when I slipped on my rubbers and my head crashed through
the boards. I couldn't free myself nor could the other players
dislodge me. A long time went past before a joiner was summoned to cut me free. In another match the ball was hit up into
the air and Hallam shouted 'Dickie' and Stanley Jayasinghe,
the Ceylonese batsman who used to play for Leicester, shouted
'Jack Birkenshaw'. Both Birky and myself carried on and
crashed into each other. I went down with an injured shoulder
which troubled me for weeks. Birky was concussed and we were
both carried off.

But there were happier times. Playing against the 1960
Springboks, Hallam and I set a record post-war Leicester opening stand of 277. Geoff Griffin, called for throwing by Sid
Buller in the Lord's Test, was playing as a batsman. I'd never
thought about umpiring up to then. I accepted the umpire's
decision and that was it. I never tried to put myself in the
umpire's position. It was obvious I was not going to be a top-
drawer county cricketer so I began to think about my future. I
enrolled for an MCC Advanced Coaching course at Lilleshall
and was one of fourteen who passed. There were some big
names who didn't make it, Alan Knott, Derek Underwood and
Bob Cottam among them.

In 1965 I asked Leicester for my release. If Ray Illingworth
had been captain and not Hallam, it might have been different.
I needed encouraging. My form had got worse and worse and
nothing I could do could change it. That year I played against
Wilfrid Isaac's XI and Wilf, a leading figure in South African
cricket, asked me if I would like to coach in South Africa during
the winter. I accepted an offer from the Transvaal Cricket
Union of £25 a week plus my keep for coaching white boys.
There were several English professionals out there, including
Mike Taylor (now with Hampshire), Derek Taylor (his twin

brother, now with Somerset), Clive Radley (Middlesex) and Bob Woolmer (Kent). Bob was a very nice lad who used to make a habit of going to the best country clubs in an old banger which kept breaking down before blowing up in the centre of Johannesburg.

In 1966 I started a summer job as a coach with the Plymouth College, a public school, and I also played as a professional with Paignton for £20 a week. Those were enjoyable summers, and in four seasons with Paignton I scored more than 10,000 runs. And it wasn't a very good square either!

My first game as a first-class umpire was on 9, 10 and 11 May, in 1970. That was the year the South Africans, most of whom I knew, were due to tour England but the tour was cancelled after the Home Secretary, Jim Callaghan, later to become Prime Minister, put pressure on the Cricket Council. I thought it would be easy to find a hotel in London but when I arrived the night before the match was scheduled to start, it was difficult to find accommodation. I forgot the Rugby League Cup Final was on!

After hours of searching, I found a place in Swiss Cottage. I booked in and discovered that I was just as nervous as I had been on my first visit to the Yorkshire nets. I asked the receptionist for a 4.30 a.m. call. I wanted to be sure of getting to the Oval on time!

By 6.30 I had arrived at the Oval, which of course was barricaded up in case of anti-apartheid demonstrators. I threw my bag over the wall and was just about to climb over when I heard a voice below: it was a policeman. I said my ball had gone over and I was retrieving it. He said, 'The next thing you'll be telling me is that you are the Prime Minister.' I showed him my official umpire's card and we had a laugh.

The other umpire was Cec Pepper, the Australian League cricketer, who was thirteen years older than me and had been on the first-class list for six years. Cec arrived at a more ortho-dox time. The first day's play was washed out, which was a big anti-climax. On the second day, the ground staff dried the square and we seemed to be ready to start except that Cec thought the light was too bad. *Wisden* described it as 'a curious assessment of the light', and I agreed. It didn't seem too bad to me. But when I told Pepper what I felt, he said, 'It's too bad and that's all there is to it.' I tried to suggest a time for starting but he replied, 'You suggest nothing. You sit there.'

Micky Stewart, the Surrey captain, was most unhappy about the delay but Brian Close, the Yorkshire captain, said he wasn't too bothered. Cec and I sat in the umpires' room on the top floor of the Oval pavilion. He smoked a big cigar and I just sat there. The *Daily Telegraph* correspondent, E. W. Swanton, knocked and entered and asked why the match hadn't started. Cec said, 'We're off because the light is bloody bad, that's why.' Mr Swanton retired.

The *Daily Mail* cricket writer, Alex Bannister, was critical of the decision and Cec took it personally when he read the morning newspapers the next day. Pepper went round to the press room next to the secretary's office but Bannister wasn't there at the time. When the match did start, the crowd was sparse and with no time for a result, there was little point in playing. It was a melancholy start to my new career. I never did find out from Cec Pepper why he didn't want to play in that match.

Our next game together was at Cambridge the next day, Cambridge University *v.* Derbyshire. We stayed in the best hotel and Cec paid all my expenses. He is a very generous man. Majid, the Cambridge captain and later Pakistan captain, scored 117 in 160 minutes. I rate him one of the best batsmen to come to England from abroad and he is a nice person with it. He has such a great knowledge of the game. When he resigned as Glamorgan captain it was said he didn't communicate but I thought he'd taught the Glamorgan youngsters a lot. He was sorely missed in Welsh cricket.

At the end of every match the two captains award the umpires marks, up to ten, and the forms are sent to Lord's where the records are kept. The umpire never knows his marks but if they were poor, it is unlikely that he would be retained on the list the following season. I never worry about marks, or trying to curry favour with captains. We have a job to do and I try to do it to the best of my ability. I may make a mistake but as Sid Buller once told me, 'Forget about it and concentrate on the next ball going down. You can't do anything about it.' Like football referees, umpires don't make mistakes because it is their opinion that counts, no-one else's. If the umpire thinks a batsman is out, he's out.

At the end of the 1970 season I had a letter from Billy Griffith, the then secretary of MCC, congratulating me on my work. That meant a lot to me. I still have the letter at home.

2

Run Out

The layman thinks the most difficult decision for an umpire to make in a Test match is leg before wicket, or perhaps caught behind down the legside. I have never been worried by leg before. The batsman has got to be 100 per cent in front for me. The most testing decision, in my view, is run out. My biggest mistake in Tests was a run out attempt by the Pakistanis in the Fifth Test at the Oval in 1974. Dennis Amiss was the batsman and I was at square leg. Dennis played the ball to the third man fence and ran. He ran one, got to the other end, turned, and decided there was a second run. I could see it was going to be tight. It was a good eighty-yard throw from Aftab Baloch, the 12th man, and Wasim Bari, the Pakistan captain against England in 1977–8, whipped the bails off as Amiss dived towards the line. It made a great sports picture for the Birmingham photographer Ken Kelly, who is one of the best cricket photographers in the business. His graphic shot of Amiss throwing himself headlong, bat outstretched, was one of a portfolio which won him a Sports Photograph of the Year award in 1974. I thought Dennis Amiss had just made it and gave him the benefit of the doubt. Remember that the law says the batsman is out of his ground unless some part of his bat or his person is grounded behind the line of the popping crease.

The umpire has much to watch out for at this point. He must be looking at the wicket keeper to see exactly at what point he gathers the ball. He has to have the stumps in his vision, to see the bails are not falling off before the wicket keeper knocks them off (some wicket keepers have been known to tap the base of the stumps with their feet). And he has to watch the bat and the popping crease.

The Pakistan opener, Sadiq Mohammed, or 'Squeaking Bill' as I call him because of his high-pitched voice, was the closest fielder. 'I wasn't sure on that one,' I said. 'You ran across me and blurred it for me.' Which was true. Sadiq had partially obstructed me. He said reassuringly, 'He was in anyway.' Normally, I don't bother about the TV replays as I am the man who has to make the decision, but this time I made a point of watching TV that night. At normal speed, the replay showed that Amiss was in. But when it was slowed down, it was apparent that Amiss was out. His bat was an inch short of the line. No-one else brought it up or criticized me. Amiss himself thought he'd made it, but I knew I had slipped up. Amiss went on to score 183 to ensure a draw for England. I worried about that mistake but it wasn't important in the context of the match. I remembered what Sid Buller used to say, 'You can't alter a decision once it's in the book.'

Being run out is an infuriating way to go, especially if the batsman knows there would have been a run in it if the correct running procedure had been used. Once in a Yorkshire League match, Barnsley v. Sheffield United, I was batting with Geoff Boycott and was 49 not out and anticipating a big collection from the large crowd for reaching my half-century. I drove the ball out to long on and shouted, 'Come one.' I was nearly at Boycott's end when I realized he hadn't budged. There was no chance of getting back because the fielder had the ball in his hand. Geoff said, 'Keep running . . . to the pavilion.'

Next to the run out, the most tricky decision for the umpire is the bat-pad catch, when the batsman gets a faint edge on to his pad and the ball rebounds to a close catcher. There is too much gamesmanship in this respect these days. Test match players will shout 'catch it' when the ball comes off the pad knowing full well the batsman hasn't touched the ball.

In the volatile atmosphere of Test cricket – crowds don't sit there sedately and orderly as they did before the last war – it is hard for an umpire to detect a nick. He has to watch for the deviation and often it is impossible to see.

Test match cricket is so pressured these days, particularly when the batting side is defending, that often there are four or five fielders in close catching positions. This never happened in the old days. Those pictures of Harold Larwood in Australia showed the short leg fielders anything up to twenty yards from the bat. Today, they can be two or three yards away.

I had an anxious day once when Ian Chappell scored his 192 for Australia against England at the Oval in 1975. Early on there was a concerted appeal for a bat-pad catch off the bowling of Phil Edmonds. I said, 'Not out.' But I wasn't happy about it and worried about it for the rest of the session. Alan Knott came up to me later in the day and said, 'You're looking a bit worried, Dickie. If it means anything to you, he didn't touch it, so stop worrying.' It made me wonder why everyone had appealed for it.

Bump ball presents problems, especially in the slip area where the umpire can be unsighted if one fielder dives across the line of another. This is where umpires must work together. It is the square leg umpire's duty to indicate whether the catch was up. I have never asked a fielder whether it was a fair catch or not because I believe I am paid to make those decisions. But there are still some players left in the game who will help you. I can think of Harry Pilling, Mike Smedley and Alan Ealham, and of course, Christopher Cowdrey, Colin's son, among quite a number.

Rod Marsh, the Australian wicket keeper, has been criticized for his apparent lack of sportsmanship but I have never had any reason to doubt him. He appeals a lot, but any fielder is entitled to appeal. He just takes it harder than most when the umpire says no. During the Centenary Test in Melbourne he called Derek Randall back after Randall had been given caught behind. That doesn't happen too often in Test cricket.

The best decision I made in Tests came in the First Test England v. India at Old Trafford in June 1974. Either side

could have won on the final day and as long as little Vishwanath was at the crease, India still had a chance. The last
twenty overs had started and he was getting behind every
delivery the England quick bowlers bowled at him. Chris Old
was bowling from the Stretford end and Vishy had just reached
his fifty. The next ball was a shortish delivery, pitched leg and
going down the legside at hip height (well, to a normal batsman
that would be somewhere between knee and thigh because
Vishy is a very small man). Vishy tried to glide it down to fine
leg. I was sure I saw the slightest deflection.

Old didn't appeal but Alan Knott held the ball up and
shouted loudly. Vishy looked appealingly at me, eyes rolling.
Usually he walks. This time he stayed his ground. 'That's out,'
I said. He turned and walked sadly away. The last five wickets
fell for 43 runs and England won by 113 runs. At the end of the
game I went to the Indian dressing-room to give Vishy his
sweater.

As I handed it to him, he said, 'So sorry, Mr Dickie, for
standing like that. It just flicked my glove but I had to stand
there because of the position we were in. I was fighting to save
my country.' I said, 'That's all right. You are entitled to stand.'
He is a lovely little fellow. Chris Old said he had no idea it was
a touch but John Edrich told me he thought it was a good
decision.

Another decision that gave me satisfaction was Greg Chappell
caught Knott bowled Old in the Fourth Test in 1975. Old
bowled Chappell an away swinger and as Chappell went to play
it, he rammed his bat hard into the ground. I was certain the
ball brushed his bat, though any noise was submerged in the
louder sound from his bat contacting the ground. I had no hesitation in giving him out. After the day's play was over I went
to the Australian dressing-room for a shower – umpires don't
have their own showers at the Oval – and I met Greg. 'I
thought I'd got away with that one,' he said with a smile. The
two incidents showed the differing philosophies of the Indian
and Australian cricketer.

I dress meticulously before every match, invariably taking

the same items to the middle with me. I suppose I am best known for my broad-fronted white cap, my trademark. I have four sent to me each season by a firm in Luton and I usually wear one if the sun is out.

Albert Modley, the Yorkshire-born music hall comedian, used to wear a similar hat. I remember seeing him when I was a boy. He had a loud booming voice and people say my voice has the same resonant qualities. Norman Wisdom also wore a cap like this and the connection with comedians might be the reason why I am looked on as something of a comic myself. Nowadays people identify me as the man with the white cap. At a reception at Clarence House during the Jubilee Test at Lord's in 1977, the Queen Mother said to me, 'I noticed on television today that you weren't wearing your white cap? What happened to it?'

I explained that it was a fairly cloudy day and I didn't wear it in those conditions. I was amazed that the Queen Mother had noticed such a small point. She must be a keen cricket watcher, I thought! I also wear a short white jacket which is the regulation style issued by Lord's and a pair of dark, charcoal grey trousers from Burton's. I have four pairs of lightweight cricket shoes which I alternate. Most cricketers today wear shoes, not boots. They are more comfortable.

I also wear a white shirt, a black tie (it looks the part) and a cricket sweater, a Leicestershire one. In my pockets I carry chewing gum (yes, I chew, I think it helps relieve the tension and keeps dryness out of the mouth), a pair of scissors, a pen-knife for cleaning mud from players' boots, a needle and cotton, safety pins, a spare ball, a rag, a spare bail and something to count with, in my case, red barrels from a brewery company. Ron Aspinall, the former Yorkshire bowler and umpire, gave me the barrels and I find them invaluable. Some umpires use coins, or pebbles. Johnny Arnold, the ex-Hampshire player, always used chestnuts from a tree in his garden. Not many umpires use the clicker. I find it clumsy.

The scissors were useful in the 1974 England v. India series when Sunil Gavaskar, the Indian opener, found that his hair

was falling into his eyes. 'Have you got any scissors, Mr Dickie?'
he said. I think he was surprised to find that I had a pair. I cut
off a few handfuls of hair and deposited them behind the stumps.
It was the first occasion that hair cutting had stopped play in a
Test match. 'I won't need to go to the barber's again this
summer,' said Gavaskar.

I usually signal distinctively, with a wide sweep of the arm.
Some people have compared me with Sir John Barbirolli, but I
believe in making myself clear at all times for the sake of the
scorer. Before each game the umpires have to test the balls with
a gauge which has two holes in it. To pass the test, the ball has
to go through one hole and not the other. This is because the
laws of the game say the ball must weigh not less than $5\frac{1}{2}$ ounces
and not more than $5\frac{3}{4}$. It is impossible for each hand-made
product to be exactly the same weight.

Technically, the umpires are supposed to measure the pitch
to see it does not exceed the laid down twenty-two yards. We go
out to inspect it but we never measure it unless there is some
doubt, because the groundsman can be relied upon to make sure
it is the correct length. I remember once when playing for
Leicestershire against Somerset at Ashby de la Zouch, Bill
Alley, opening the bowling for Somerset, suddenly said after
bowling the first ball, which, incidentally, was a long hop, 'Hey,
this pitch is too long. I've never bowled a long hop in my life!'
Hugo Yarnold was one of the umpires. We were all surprised
but the umpires thought Bill was justified and we trooped off
while the groundsman came out with his chain to measure. It
was found that the pitch was twenty-four yards long!

Ashby is now no longer a county ground, which pleases the
players. It is a pretty ground but in those days lacked any refine-
ments. There was just one shower and one toilet between the
twenty-two players and two umpires, and birds' nests were
everywhere. Once the Surrey team refused to change there.
Micky Stewart, the Surrey captain, made his players change in
their hotel and walk to the ground.

The umpires must make sure the pitch is not abused. One
dodge that players get up to is to keep tapping the pitch and

brushing it with their bats as though there are loose bits of earth that need removing. Whenever I see this happening, I intervene. That is the quickest way to knock the top off a pitch, especially on the last day.

There was once an occasion when a batsman admitted in the pub after the end of the day's play that he had been caught off the last ball of the day but no-one appealed. When the match resumed the next day, one of the fielders appealed, insisting that he was allowed an appeal according to the laws of the game before an over starts. The umpire had to give the batsman out. Since then, umpires have to call 'Time' at the end of the day which effectively concludes all matters relating to that day's cricket.

In the Yorkshire v. Sussex match at Headingley in 1976 Geoff Cope was bowling to John Spencer when the ball jumped up and caught wicket keeper David Bairstow between the eyes. It rebounded to gully, where Bill Athey held it. Colin Kay, the Yorkshire physiotherapist, came on to stick plaster on the cut on Bairstow's head and I called 'over' and changed over to square leg for Chris Old to bowl the first ball of his next over. Phil Carrick was fielding there and as Chris bowled the ball he whispered in my ear, 'How's that?' I said, 'What are you appealing for?' Said Carrick, 'That last ball. It hit the bat first.' I replied, 'It's too late now, it's all finished.'

But at the end of the over I asked Carrick why he had appealed and he said, 'Your mate at the other end, Don Oslear, told me to.' I think he was testing me out. The fielder is entitled to appeal before the over starts. But Old had already bowled one delivery.

One of the most controversial incidents in Tests concerning time came in the West Indies v. England Test at Port of Spain in 1973-4 when Tony Greig threw down the stumps at Alvin Kallicharran's end as the players began to walk off the field. Strictly according to the laws, because the umpire hadn't called time, Greig was right but it was against the spirit of the game and the decision that Kallicharran was run out was quite properly reversed.

There are eighteen pages of small type in the laws of the game as published in *Wisden* and a further six pages of regulations. It is a lot of words to digest, especially as they are in semi-legal phraseology. Not many players bother to read the laws too closely which is why there are always little disputes when there need not be.

Boundaries are another source of contention. It is the duty of the umpires to check boundaries before play. At Lord's, for instance, not many people realize that if a batsman hits the ball into the wire fence under the Father Time Stand without bouncing it is a four, not a six. Likewise the little wall in front of the pavilion. If the ball hits it, then we are supposed to signal four. Only if the ball clears the wall is it a six. The umpires and captains always get together before the start of a match to agree to this.

There are some players who know the laws intimately and I number among them Mike Brearley, Ray Illingworth and Tony Brown. Most of the others pick it up as they go along. Players make mistakes and though I always say umpires never do, there are times when we make a simple human error. In a Yorkshire *v*. Kent county championship match at Bramall Lane we were having lunch when Ted Lester, the Yorkshire scorer, said, 'Do you know you've given a seven-baller?'

David Constant, who was standing with me, said with a big laugh, 'Bad luck, old boy.' Lester said to him, 'You shut up. You've given one and all.' My most memorable alleged seven-baller came in the Trent Bridge Test against the West Indies in 1976. Wayne Daniel was bowling and it was a rather eventful over. David Steele was allegedly caught by Andy Roberts at long leg hooking a bouncer from Daniel off the seventh ball of that over. I say allegedly because that was what Bill Frindall, the BBC radio statistician, told the commentators at the time and afterwards some journalists came to question me about it.

What happened was that earlier in the over Daniel bowled a wide and as he followed through, he came down the line of the middle stump in the prohibited zone which bowlers are supposed to avoid. In my anxiety to make sure Daniel was warned

I forgot to signal the wide properly. I half stretched both arms without actually facing the scorers to make clear my intentions. I was too busy asking Clive Lloyd to come over to receive the final warning. The players knew I had called 'wide'.

'If he runs down the pitch again, Clive, he'll have to come off,' I said. Lloyd said, 'Can you nurse him?' I replied, 'What more can I do?' At the time, Daniel was all over the place, no-balling, bowling wides and running down the pitch. But he straightened himself out by the end of the summer and in 1977, while playing for Middlesex in the championship, gave the umpires no trouble.

The scorers realized my slip-up in not signalling the wide properly and so had Fred Trueman in the radio box. Tommy Spencer, the other umpire, also knew it was a wide. But next day the public were told that Steele was out to the seventh ball of an over!

The front foot law is not an easy one to enforce. The umpire has to watch the back foot on the return crease, the front foot, the batsman at the other end and the bowler running down the pitch, but I think it is much preferable to the old back foot law. I think it is a good law even though the Australians don't like it.

I have yet to call a bowler for throwing. If we think a bowler is suspect – and there have been several suspect bowlers in recent times – we make a report to the Test and County Cricket Board who make arrangements for the bowler concerned to be filmed in secret. I would have no hesitation in no-balling an offender but it hasn't happened to me in seven years.

I have only once seen a case of batsman out handled the ball. It happened in South Africa and the batsman was Graeme Pollock ¨playing for Eastern Province v. Western Province at Newlands. Graeme played forward and the ball went up into the air off his pad and shoulder. The wicket keeper said, 'Leave it, it's going to bowl him.' The ball was dropping on the stumps when Pollock turned and knocked it away. He didn't like it when he was given out. Rodney Cass, the former Essex and Worcester wicket keeper, once got away with a rare piece of audacity in South Africa in another match. He appeared to be bowled but picked the bails up and put them back on, explaining that the wind had blown them off. No-one argued and he continued his innings.

'Hit wicket' doesn't pose many problems. The batsman knows when he is out. An outstanding example was in the World Cup Final at Lord's in 1975 when Roy Fredericks played a fantastic hook shot against a bouncer from Dennis Lillee, but in doing so he trod on his wicket. He didn't have to be given out. He walked away sadly. Nor, as I have said, does lbw worry me. A factor I take into account is where the bowler is bowling from. If he bowls close to the stumps I give his appeal more sympathy than the appeal of a bowler bowling wide of the stumps. The odds are that the wider the bowler comes in, the greater the chance the ball will go down the legside. I look for the ball to hold its course. If it starts cutting back or swinging towards leg, I usually give the batsman the benefit. It has to be hitting the stumps to be out.

Stumpings are taxing, more so when the line is being worn away and it is not easy to pick it out. One umpire, Peter Rochford, the former Gloucester wicket keeper, once told me he thought some stumpings were so fast they deceived the eye and I believe him. He instanced the case of Denis Compton in a match at Bristol. Sam Cook, also an umpire, was bowling and Denis went down the pitch to drive and missed. Rochford whipped the bails off and Sid Buller said, 'Not out.'

But Compton turned to Rochford and said, 'I was out. You were too quick for him.' The fastest stumper I ever saw was Farokh Engineer of India and Lancashire. He too said he was too quick for umpires. 'Rookie' was so lightning fast that sometimes it was not easy to tell whether he had taken the bails off fairly. You had the impression he had knocked them off with his gloves before he gathered the ball. When this happened once in a match I said, 'Put them back on and get on with the game, Rookie.' He laughed. He always enjoyed his cricket.

There was only one time I can remember calling a batsman back. It was in a Sussex v. Middlesex match at Hove in 1970, my first year on the list. The batsman was Jim Parks. John

'Sport' Price was bowling to Peter Graves and Graves drove straight back at him.

Price got a touch to the ball and it hit the stumps. In the split second that followed, Parks went out of his ground looking for a run. There was an appeal and I signalled out. Parks walked away, not saying anything. Then I realized that at the moment the wicket was broken, Parks was still in his ground. He left it after the bails came off.

I went to Mike Brearley, who was then captaining Middlesex in his first season as skipper, and said, 'I am sorry but I am going to call Jim Parks back. I made a mistake.' Brearley took it sportingly. 'You're correct,' he said.

3
Cheating

The first experience I had of cheating in cricket came when I was in my teens and playing for Barnsley in the Yorkshire League. Cheating always has been a part of cricket and, as long as there are laws to try and get round, always will be. One of the niftiest exponents of removing the bails before the ball arrived and making it look as though the batsman was stumped was a League cricketer named Bill Lilley. He was a local hero in the district and a first-class wicket keeper.

Bill used to fix a hair pin in his boot in such a manner that he could flick the base of the stumps and disturb the bails. He once did it to me but I said, 'Come on, Bill, put those bails back on.' In one match, Mitchell's Main v. Cortonwood in the Yorkshire Council League, Bill did it to a fellow named Fred Robinson, who was a driving examiner. Fred wasn't very happy when he found out how he had been dismissed. In the bar afterwards some of the players discovered that Bill Lilley was due to under-go his driving test on the Monday . . . and the examiner was Fred Robinson. Bill Lillee never did turn up for that driving test! He cancelled the appointment and took it later at Don-caster.

Illegal shining of the ball is a sharp practice which is still prevalent at all levels of the game despite attempts by umpires to stop it. Players apply lip salve, or some other colourless fluid to the ball to keep the shine on.

During one Test in the England v. Australia series in 1975

I thought I smelt something suspicious on Dennis Lillee's
sweater. It wasn't the smell of pure wool or whatever they make
sweaters from these days. I said to him, 'Are you using oil on this
ball?' He said, 'I'm too good a bowler to do that!' We laughed
about it. There is no way of proving that an offence has been
committed short of having an on the spot laboratory test. Experimental Law 46 explicitly prohibits interference with the ball by
use of wax, resin or any other substance but I often marvel at
the condition of some balls after 85 overs.

The bowler invariably says he's done it by applying sweat
and working hard at it on his trousers but one side will be
blood red and the other rough through normal wear. I say to
the bowler, 'How is this ball as red as this?' And he usually
replies, 'It's only sweat, Dickie.' In the Somerset v. Australians
match at Bath I noticed that Mick Malone, the swing bowler,
had sun cream plastered all over his nose in a most conspicuous
way. I said to him, 'What's the matter? What's that you've got
on your nose?'

He replied, 'It's sun cream. I've put it on to protect my nose
from the sun.' 'Sun?' I said. 'I don't see any sun. It looks like
rain.' The ball never swung all day. I let the bowler know I
suspect something early on and then I find he doesn't infringe
the law. I often smell the ball. It is a pointed way of saying 'I'm
watching you.'

One way of carrying the oil or cream on to the field is to apply
it to the lips and then transfer it by the tips of the fingers to the
ball. I once remember seeing Mike Buss, the Sussex all-rounder,
wiping his lips in a peculiar manner in one match. 'Here, what
are you doing?' I said. 'My lips are very sore,' he said. 'I suffer
from sore lips.' I had to make sure the ball wasn't getting the
same treatment as his lips.

Does illegal shining make all that difference? It can do, in the
right conditions. In South Africa, lots of bowlers use lip ice and
seem to be able to get away with it. South African bowlers lead
the world in the art of shining. Their umpires are not strict
enough about it. The South Africans also use the Kookaburra
ball, which is supposed to swing more. It was used in a small

number of matches in England but I am not convinced that it swings any more than our own balls.

Fred Trueman used to be a dedicated polisher of the ball (I mean in the legal sense because the bowler is allowed to rub the ball on his flannels or shirt). But I don't think even Fred at his best could beat the Australian, Max Walker. Max really works on the ball and usually manages to swing it no matter what the conditions. A contemporary in English cricket who comes near the top of the list as a star polisher is Mike Taylor of Hampshire. These chaps must have astronomical laundry bills!

In one match I was playing at Taunton, Ken Palmer pitched a ball on leg stump and it removed my middle stump. Something extraordinary had to happen to make the ball do that because in those days Taunton was a featherbed – it still is a good batting wicket – and the ball hadn't moved off the pitch all day. Years later, I was umpiring a match with Ken and he showed me how he did it: he raised the seam of the ball by flicking his thumb nail round it. I was amazed at how quickly he did it. If the ball pitched on the upraised seam, anything could happen.

Nowadays there isn't so much of this going on. Umpires regularly inspect the ball and would soon find out what was happening. But in the old days, it was a commonplace event. John Shepherd, the Kent seam bowler, says it doesn't make any difference but my experience at Taunton has convinced me that it does! The relevant law says, 'It is illegal for a player to lift the seam of the ball in order to obtain a better hold. In such a case the umpire will, if necessary, change the ball for one which has had similar wear and will warn the captain that the practice is unfair.'

A relatively new 'offence' is encroachment by fielders in an effort to unsettle batsmen. We were getting a situation where fielders were standing on the edge of the pitch and moving their arms about as the bowler bowled. Tony Greig was, I believe, guilty of this on occasions. In 1975 the authorities introduced an experimental law in the section 'Fair and Unfair Play.' It read, 'An umpire is justified in intervening under this law

should any player of the fielding side incommode the striker by
any noise or motion while he is receiving a ball. Whilst the ball
is in play and until the ball has made contact with the bat or
the striker's person or has passed the bat, no fieldsman, other
than the bowler, may stand on or have any part of his person
extended over the cut portion of the pitch (area 22 yards by 10
feet). In the event of infringement the umpire shall call and
signal No Ball.'

The year before, in the England v. India Test Greig was
fielding so close to Sunil Gavaskar on the offside that I thought
I ought to intervene even though the law was not in general use.
When Gavaskar got to my end, I said, 'Is this fellow Tony Greig
bothering you there? Is he too close?' Said Sunny, 'Keep quiet,
Dickie! That's a fielder wasted. He is too close to catch me.'
Gavaskar was laying back and square cutting Underwood, and
Greig was continually having to jump out of the way. If Greig
had been in a normal position he would have saved many runs.
I never saw Greig make a catch in that position.

One of the first occasions when the new experimental law was
invoked was a match involving Middlesex. Fred Titmus, who
was in his last days with Middlesex, bowled and Norman
Featherstone, fielding very close, made the catch. The batsman
started to walk off. Don Oslear, the umpire, said, 'No ball.'
Titmus was annoyed. 'What do you mean?' he said. 'I've never
bowled a no ball in my life.' Oslear explained that the fielder
was too close and that was why he was calling a no ball.

Time wasting is another offence which the authorities have
tried to stamp out. Since the Brian Close case at Edgbaston in
1967, when Close was censured for deliberately wasting time,
there has been a crackdown which has generally been successful.
Umpires are empowered to warn the bowler for taking an un-
necessarily long time to bowl an over and if that warning is
ineffective, they can order the captain to take the bowler off and
the bowler cannot bowl again in the innings. I have never yet
had to use these powers. I find a few words early on usually
suffice. No bowler wants to be debarred from bowling.

Judging whether the light is good enough for play to continue, particularly in Test matches which tend these days to be dominated by bowlers of extreme pace, is one of the hardest parts of umpiring. I don't enjoy this and I wish a way could be found to take the responsibility out of the umpire's hands. You try to be fair and honest but it is impossible to please everyone. Players will put pressure on you by making remarks but you can't let that worry you.

We were strongly criticized, Tommy Spencer and myself, in the England v. West Indies Test at Nottingham in 1976, over light. There was one day when it seemed to be on the borderline most of the day. Trent Bridge isn't the best of grounds for visibility, particularly from the pavilion end. We had the added annoyance of a nine-minute hold-up when some drunken West Indian supporters broke into the enclosure while Viv Richards and Alvin Kallicharran were batting and caused a disturbance.

Many people couldn't understand the reasons for the delay because it was not clear what was going on. But Viv declared he couldn't continue with people moving about behind the arm and I went over to ask the spectators to settle down. Some West Indians were fighting, the worst scenes I can recall at a Test in England. I asked a policeman if he could go in and restore order but he said, 'Not likely. I might get knifed.' When the situation was calmed and play resumed, the light deteriorated and I could have been killed when Richards drove a ball straight back down the wicket. It whistled past me for four but I didn't see it. I thought it was time to bring them in! Crowds don't understand light rulings. Often they say the players have gone in when the light has improved, not understanding that the pace of the bowlers has to be considered.

These days the batsman has no right of appeal against the light. The decision is left to the umpires who, after a conference, can 'offer the opportunity of going in' to the batsmen. If the batsmen are going well, it is unlikely they will want their concentration broken. Many a stand in Tests has been ended when players have gone in and then come out again a few minutes later.

Once the batsmen have elected to go on in bad light they are allowed an appeal if they change their minds about continuing. But the umpires have to be sure the light is much worse before going in. Personally, I wish some kind of light meter could be devised to take this onerous task away from umpires. It causes more unrest and rows than almost anything else. Whatever decision the umpires make, it is sure to upset someone.

That Trent Bridge Test was the scene of another bewildering incident when Gordon Greenidge, opening the West Indies second innings with Roy Fredericks and needing to score quick runs, asked for a runner. He was suffering from a leg strain. Tony Greig, the England captain, objected as Collis King, the player sent out to run, wasn't in the West Indies twelve. I think there may have been a misunderstanding and that some of us may have felt King was the 12th man. A wag said that, in the prevailing light, the West Indians all looked the same. They kept coming on and off all day. It was hard to see who was who under their caps.

Greig probably objected because he thought King was one of the fastest runners in the West Indies party but according to the laws, the fielding captain has no say about who runs, although he can have a say in who fields as a substitute and where the substitute *can't* field. For example, if the replacement fielder is a brilliant slip fielder, the captain can tell him not to field in the slips.

As I told the players, anyone can run for a batsman, even Clyde Walcott, the West Indies manager, and the fielding side couldn't do anything about it. Law 2 is quite clear about this point.

There was further confusion in that Test because the West Indies' 12th man and others were continually running out to take over from fielders. They seemed to have had a lot of people wanting to go to the toilet suddenly in that particular match. Eventually it was decided that King could not be used and Larry Gomes came out as Greenidge's runner. Greenidge only made 23 before being caught and bowled by Old and Gomes wasn't out in the middle long. Afterwards, the batsmen objected when Chris Old, struck earlier by Andy Roberts, bowled with a strapping on his arm. They said it was putting them off so Old had to bowl with his sleeves rolled down.

Most cricketers cheat at some time or other, however high their moral values. There comes a time when 'a walker' stands his ground, as happened to Vishwanath in that Test at Old Trafford. It happened to me once in a Leicestershire Second XI match. When I was on 25, the ball barely touched my glove, and bounced into short leg's hands off the thigh pad. I was given not out and went on to make 100. No-one said anything about it afterwards though I did feel rather guilty!

Other than that one incident, I have always walked myself. There aren't many batsmen these days who stand their ground. More walk than not. Colin Cowdrey was one and I had great respect for him. Frank Hayes is another. But there is nothing in the laws about a batsman having to give himself up if there is some doubt. He cannot reverse an umpire's decision if he has been wrongly given out. If players are prepared to walk, well, I admire them. If they don't, then I do not blame them too much. It is their living, after all.

Umpires are told to intervene in cases of bad behaviour or offensive comment on the field by players, but this rarely happens. Most matches are played in a good spirit. Of course players swear and curse – it is a very competitive game and passions can easily be roused. I do not think the problem of bad language is any worse than it used to be.

Perhaps I have been lucky but I have not been involved in any cases of extreme bad behaviour on the field. I believe in cracking a joke or two and calming people down. Sometimes bowlers, particularly pace bowlers, will abuse the batsmen as they are following through down the pitch. It is an occupational pursuit of the fast bowler.

If I hear it, I will say, 'Hey, what's going on there? That's enough of that!' This system seems to work. I cannot see a case for a soccer-style system of showing yellow cards to players and booking them. Umpires have the power to stop a bowler from bowling if warnings are ignored and no bowler likes not being allowed to bowl.

It is said that the Australians, with their 'sledging' or pointed comments at batsmen in an effort to needle them, are difficult for an umpire to handle but I must say I haven't had too many problems with them myself. I get on well with them, as I will explain later.

I have never come across an instance of a player showing dissent with any of my decisions. If there had been such a case, I would have reported it to Lord's. I think I may have been lucky. I seem to have a good understanding of the players and we never reach a point where we have to exchange words.

English cricket has fortunately been free of examples of dissent. Just about the only known case of a player being disciplined for this offence was the Geoff Arnold affair in 1974. Arnold was found guilty of showing 'public dissent' against a decision of Peter Wight in a John Player League match between Warwickshire and Surrey at Edgbaston on 21 July. Wight signalled a wide and the bowler was alleged to have made a petulant gesture.

When the case came before the Test and County Cricket Board's Disciplinary Committee, Arnold, who was in the England side at the time, was suspended for two matches. I have never had any trouble with Geoff Arnold myself. He is a wholehearted bowler who, like many pace bowlers, sometimes has a curse to himself when things go against him.

4

Bouncers

The mistake I made was to hit Frank Tyson's first three deliveries for four. I might have known the next ball in that match at Scarborough would be a bouncer. As he bowled it, Frank said, 'Hit that bastard for four.'

I was half on the front foot, looking to drive again, when the ball smashed into the side of my jaw and knocked me to the ground. There was blood all over my face and inside my mouth. I was dazed but not completely out. Faintly, I could hear the 'ting, ting, ting' of the ambulance. People seemed to be laughing. I was carried off the field and lifted into the ambulance. At the hospital, the X-ray showed that my jaw wasn't broken but the wound needed a stitch or two. I was patched up and went back to resume my innings.

At the time Tyson was probably the fastest bowler in England. Not long before, he'd earned the nickname 'Typhoon' in Australia as he demolished the Australian batsmen in the 1954–5 series. He was very fast, but not as fast as Holding or Thomson.

I had encountered bouncers before but that was the first one that had really maimed me. Tyson never apologized. Norman Yardley, the former Yorkshire captain and a member of the committee, said it was my own fault, I should have expected a bouncer. I should have been on the back foot. We were tough in those Yorkshire days.

The other time I was hit on the head was against Hampshire at Ilkley. Butch White bowled a reasonable bouncer in his day and this particular one struck me a glancing blow on the head and went on to bounce off the top of the sightscreen. The umpire signalled four leg byes. I sank to my knees, more in shock than pain and Willie Watson, who was batting with me at the time, said sternly, 'Get up and get on with it. You're all right.'

I might have lost some teeth on another occasion when Lancashire's Colin Hilton bounced one at me in a county match which saw Leicester bowled out for 38 on a dicey wicket. I played it down in front of my face off the knuckle part of the glove, fracturing one of the small bones in my hand.

Perhaps the most serious case of a bouncer injuring a batsman was the Charlie Griffith v. Nari Contractor incident in Barbados when Contractor, the Indian opening batsman, was on the danger list for a week after ducking into a Griffith bouncer. Contractor had a steel plate put in his head and I've been told is still troubled by it today.

Some people are very unlucky. Tom Pugh, once the Gloucester captain, ducked into a bouncer which never got up and was given out lbw. He would have retired hurt anyway because the blow fractured his jawbone. The worst incident I ever saw was in a match at Paignton, when Jeff Tolchard, now with Leicester, was hit in the face by a local bowler. His glasses were smashed and bits of glass went into his eye. He was lucky not to suffer more permanent damage.

The bouncer is a dangerous ball but it is part of the game and I would never agree with those who say it should be outlawed. It is a legitimate part of the fast bowler's armoury. Without it, the game would be much less exciting. Some of the most dramatic moments in Test cricket come when a bowler drops it short and the batsman hooks it spectacularly for four. West Indians and Australians, brought up on hard, fast wickets, usually rise to the challenge. To stop bowlers bowling bouncers to someone like Clive Lloyd would rob the game of one of its finest sights.

The trouble comes when bowlers start peppering the batsmen with bouncers and the bouncer becomes an intimidating weapon. This happened, apparently, on the final session's play in the England v. West Indies Test at Old Trafford in 1976

when Mike Holding, Andy Roberts and Wayne Daniel overdid
it against Brian Close and John Edrich. Edrich felt so upset
about it that he said later he felt like coming off the field.
'Surely cricket hasn't come to this,' he said.

Many deliveries flew over their heads and only 21 runs were
scored in eighty minutes. Several times Close was hit about the
body and arms as he stood there, often not trying to avoid the
ball. Eventually, Bill Alley had a word with the West Indians
and later Lloyd admitted his bowlers had bowled badly and had
got carried away. There was to be no repetition.

The matter is adequately covered in the laws. The relevant
section says, 'The persistent bowling of fast short-pitched balls
is unfair if, in the opinion of the umpire at the bowler's end, it
constitutes a systematic attempt at intimidation. In such event,
he must adopt the following procedure:

(a) When he decides that such bowling is becoming persistent
he forthwith cautions the bowler.

(b) If this caution is ineffective, he informs the captain of the
fielding side and the other umpire what has occurred.

(c) Should the above prove ineffective, the umpire at the
bowler's end must:

   (i) At the first repetition call 'Dead ball' when the over is
   regarded as completed.

   (ii) Direct the captain of the fielding side to take the
   bowler off forthwith. The captain shall take the
   bowler off as directed.

   (iii) Report the occurrence to the captain of the batting
   side as soon as the interval of play takes place. A
   bowler who has been taken off as above may not bowl
   again during the same innings.

I gave a final warning to Keith Boyce, the West Indian
bowler, in the 1973 Lord's Test against England, and Boyce
soon stopped it. He was bowling two and three bouncers an
over and England's batsmen didn't like it. Boyce took 8–99 in
that match and was the tourists' leading wicket taker in the
series with 19 at 15.47 apiece. He was quick and straight and

bowled a menacing bouncer. He had a knee injury later and never bowled as fast again.

At the end of play on the Saturday he set a trap to try and dismiss Geoff Boycott, moving Alvin Kallicharran more square and bowling a bouncer. Boycott, who never normally hooks, looked round, had a little smile and fell right into it. His shot went straight to Kallicharran. Kalli didn't have to move a foot. It went straight in. That was the day when Boycott was jostled by West Indian supporters as he left the pitch and he waved his bat about angrily.

Also in that match I warned Bob Willis for overdoing the short stuff. Significantly, Gary Sobers whispered to me, 'Let him bounce them. I like it!'

Just before the First Test in 1976 I did the Sussex v. West Indies match at Hove and Wayne Daniel bowled four short-pitched balls in an over to Arnold Long, the Sussex wicket keeper. Long was struck painfully on the body and was very unhappy about it.

At the end of the over I warned Daniel and he nodded in acceptance. He is a very agreeable man, not like the popular impression of a fast bowler. He was overstepping and running down the pitch as well. In those days, he hadn't sorted his run up out. He was very raw. He didn't take any notice when I first spoke to him so I said I was giving him the official warning.

Clyde Walcott, the West Indies manager, and Deryck Murray, who was leading the side in that match, came to see me at the close of play. Clyde asked, 'What number of bouncers is allowable?' I said, 'We are not cutting out bouncers but there has to be a happy medium. Three or four an over is too many.' With the first Test starting two days later they wanted to know the position on bouncers.

In July, the subject was discussed by the International Cricket Conference meeting at Lord's. Some countries, particularly the Indians who had suffered at the hands of the West Indian bowlers in the Caribbean the year before, wanted a tough line taken but the Conference thought the existing Law 46 was sufficient and gave full backing to umpires who implemented it. In a statement, the Conference defined the short-pitched ball as one that pitches short and passes on or above shoulder height to the batsman standing normally at the crease.

The Conference also decided that the short-pitched delivery at tailenders was not in the best interests of the game and should be discontinued. When the Packer matches were announced in Australia, the organizers said bouncers would be permitted against tailenders. I agree with the ICC. A bouncer against a batsman with limited technique can be a lethal delivery.

One bowler I warned about bouncing excessively to a tailender was Mike Procter. The match was Essex v. Gloucester at Cheltenham and the batsman was Ray East. One of the many bouncers Procter bowled touched East's nose and blood spurted out. There was an appeal for a catch behind, incidentally, which I turned down!

East said, 'As a number 8, I regard myself as a tailender.' He was right, though he has scored a first-class hundred. But I would still have warned Procter because he bowled too many short deliveries. East being a tailender was irrelevant. I would have taken the same action if the batsman had been Barry Richards, Viv Richards or any other leading player.

Dennis Lillee bowls a very hostile bouncer. I define a good bouncer as one aimed towards the head which the batsman has difficulty in avoiding. If it is wide of the batsman, he doesn't have to move. The tricky one is the delivery, not all that short, which keeps coming and the batsman is in two minds. Andy Roberts, with his changes of pace, is a leading practitioner in this department of the game. He has several kinds of bouncer ranging from a medium fast one to a very fast one.

I once asked Len Hutton who bowled the best bouncer in his day. 'Keith Miller,' he said. 'He bowled a wicked bouncer.' Reg Simpson of that era probably played bouncers better than any English batsman. He kept his eyes on the ball and swayed inside the line.

The serious injuries are nearly always caused when the batsman takes his eye off the ball and backs away. If it is a right arm over the wicket bowler, the ball will tend to follow him. Keeping your eyes on the ball is all important.

I feel sympathy for batsmen who have had to withstand a lot of short-pitched bowling. Hutton was a target for it in the fifties and recently we have seen Dennis Amiss, Keith Fletcher, John Edrich and Brian Close all undergo a battering. Some, including David Lloyd of Lancashire, Fletcher and to a lesser extent Amiss, were virtually destroyed by it as Test match players. It is easy to criticize, but how many batsmen really like having the ball whizzing round their ears?

During the 1974 tour by the Indians I was with Fred Trueman when we met Lt-Col Hemu Adhikari, the former Indian Test player who was managing the side. Adhikari was one of Fred's victims in that Test at Headingley when India lost their first four wickets without scoring a single run. He backed to square leg when Fred's first delivery whistled past. His face was deathly white. Fred, introduced to him in the Old Trafford bar, said, 'Hello, Colonel. Glad to see you've got your colour back.'

Maurice Leyland used to say, 'No-one likes facing fast bowling but you should keep quiet about it and don't let on.' If a batsman shows he is worried about bouncers, the bowler will be tempted to bowl more at him. If he hooks them for six, the bowler will soon stop bowling them.

I was 12th man for Yorkshire when we met the 1959 Indian touring side at Bramall Lane. Fred was then in his prime and none of the Indian batsmen were too keen to face him. On the morning of the match, Polly Umrigar, one of the best Indian players, suddenly developed a mysterious back injury and said he wouldn't be able to play.

Word reached the Indian dressing-room that Fred was suffering from ankle trouble and might not play himself. A few minutes later, it was confirmed that Fred had failed a test. Polly Umrigar felt his back and said perhaps he could play after all. In the other dressing-room, Fred was being persuaded to play. The physio strapped up his ankle and Fred said he would turn out after all. The message was conveyed to the

Indian dressing-room. Umrigar had an immediate relapse and declared himself unfit!

During the 1974–5 tour by England of Australia, Thomson and Lillee bowled a large quota of bouncers at the English batsmen and this played a crucial part in deciding the series. Thomson interspersed the short lifter with his 'sandshoe crusher', the ball aimed at the batsman's foot. It was designed to get Tony Greig, with his high backlift, out and it often worked.

In the 1975 World Cup match against Sri Lanka at the Oval, a match I was not officiating in, he struck Wettimuny, the Sri Lankan batsman, three times on the foot and after the third time, Wettimuny was carried off and taken to hospital. Wettimuny was hobbling around outside his crease, feeling his injured foot, when Thomson picked the ball up and shied down the stumps. Wettimuny was not out because no Australian appealed. Technically, according to the laws, he would have been out if there had been an appeal.

Shortly afterwards, Thomson bowled a lifter at Duleep Mendis and Mendis was laid out by a blow on the head. As he lay on the ground, the tiny Mendis looked up at the Australians and said, 'I go now.' He went to hospital too!

The best hookers in my experience are Lloyd, Viv Richards, Alvin Kallicharran, Gary Sobers, Mushtaq Mohammed, Ian and Greg Chappell, Peter Burge and Keith Stackpole. Ian Chappell was once persuaded to cut out the hook shot because it was getting him out but it reduced his run output so much that he soon took it up again. There are no English or Indian batsmen in my list. Batsmen from these countries don't get enough practice against the short ball bouncing from a hard pitch. Uneven bounce at many English grounds makes the hook a risky shot. Colin Milburn was a fine hooker and his Northamptonshire colleague, David Steele, had some success with it before it started letting him down in Tests. Unlike Milburn, Steele wasn't a natural hooker.

Nobby Clark, the former Northampton bowler whom I meet occasionally in the summer, was a fast bowler who liked using the bouncer before the War. He was playing once against Nottinghamshire and in those days both Harold Larwood and Bill Voce were in the Nottingham team.

Nobby bowled bouncers at both Larwood and Voce. Larwood said, 'Your turn will come.' Nobby didn't believe it. He wasn't in the same class as Larwood as a batsman. But when Northampton batted and it was Nobby's turn to go in, Larwood greeted him with a bouncer which whistled past his nose. The ball flicked the outside edge of his bat and first slip caught it on the bounce. Nobby took his gloves off and started walking. 'Well bowled, Lol,' he said.

'That didn't carry,' said Larwood. 'Oh yes it did,' said Nobby. The umpire tried to call him back . . . in vain.

One of the bravest examples of a batsman being hurt and then going out to face the flak again in the same match was Colin Cowdrey's trip to the crease in the final minutes of the 1963 Test against the West Indies at Lord's. Colin had a bone broken in his arm by a bouncer in the first innings and to save the game, he went out with his arm in plaster in the second innings, prepared to bat left-handed if necessary. Colin was picked for the 1974-5 tour of Australia because he was such a good player against fast bowling and he designed a chest protector to minimize injury if he edged the ball on to his body or missed it completely.

I think a chest protector can be useful but I cannot agree with those who say cricketers should wear headgear. I cannot see headguards of the type used by England captain Mike Brearley and Dennis Amiss being universally adopted, however comfortable they may be. I see them as a handicap. All sport has a risk attached to it and cricketers have their bats and their eyes and judgement of when to let the ball go to protect them from serious injury.

Most injuries happen when the batsman tries to hook and edges the ball into his face. Often it is the front of the face that is hit and short of having a motor cyclist's headguard complete with visor, there is no way of stopping that.

5
Beamer!

The last ball before tea on the Monday of the 1974 Test between England and Pakistan at the Oval caused more controversy than any delivery I have ever had sent down from my end. It was a beamer – cricket's killer ball! A beamer is a head-high full toss and cricketers fear it more than any bouncer. It is difficult to pick up as its flight path is usually downward, which means it is very hard to duck under it. The bouncer is easier to avoid because it is going up. The beamer goes the other way.

The Oval beamer was bowled by Sarfraz Nawaz at Tony Greig. It was very fast and very straight. Greig managed to duck out of the way, a considerable feat for someone of his immense height. He was furious. He started to come down the pitch towards Sarfraz and said, 'I am going to wrap this bat round your head.'

Sarfraz, hands on hips, said, 'I am waiting for you.' In a flash I whipped the bails off and stepped between them saying, 'That's tea, gentlemen.' I urged both of them to calm down. The other players were turning away to go towards the pavilion and Sarfraz and Greig joined them.

As Sarfraz walked off I went with him. 'I want no more of those beamers, please,' I said. 'All right,' he replied. 'I am so sorry.' I also had a word with Intikhab, the Pakistan captain, asking him to speak to Sarfraz. Inti said he would.

I spoke to Greig as well and he said, 'Thanks for the way you handled that situation.' I think I was a little lucky. As it was tea, I was able to get the players away from the scene. If it had happened in the middle of an over, I might have had more problems. Both men were plainly very angry indeed.

I have spoken to Greig several times since about that incident and each time he said, 'You know, you saved my career then. The way I felt, I was going to hit him over the head with my bat.' If he'd done that, he would never have played for England again. Nor would he have gone on to captain England.

Wisden's description of the incident was, 'The following ball, a beamer, flew past Greig's head without bouncing. The two glared at each other but umpire Bird moved quickly to restrain the bowler, who was advised to calm down.' Actually, it was Greig who needed to be controlled first, not Sarfraz! It had been a frustrating day for the Pakistan bowlers. Facing a Pakistan first innings total of 600–7 declared, England began the day at 293–4 and were intent only on holding out.

Amiss, 178 not out, mishooked against Sarfraz and was hit on the cheekbone. He retired to have an X-ray which showed no bone damage. Rain had held up play, adding to the frustration. Keith Fletcher came in and played a typical rearguard innings, frequently stopping the bowlers because of movement in the crowd. This has always been a problem at the Oval, particularly at the Vauxhall end when a temporary stand is erected.

In that last over, Fletcher stopped Sarfraz again and Sarfraz threw the ball down angrily. His next delivery was a fast full toss which Fletcher turned for a single. Then came the beamer at Greig. The next day, after England saved the match, Sarfraz went to the England dressing-room to apologize.

Greig was reported to have said to him, 'What happened? You could have killed me!' And Sarfraz's answer was, 'I am very sorry. I didn't realize it was you. I was angry at the way Keith Fletcher kept pulling away when I came up to bowl. I hadn't noticed that you had crossed for a single and I thought it was still Fletcher I was bowling at. I know I shouldn't have done it but I lost my head and I am sorry.'

Greig said, 'That's okay, have a drink.' It was a perfectly

natural mistake to make. Greig is six feet seven inches tall, whereas Fletcher is about five feet ten!

I get on well with Sarfraz. He has a lively sense of humour and is one of the leading characters in the present-day game. He is not as fast as the fastest West Indian or Australian bowlers but is probably the fastest bowler ever produced by Pakistan. He can be pretty quick at times.

The other beamer incident I was involved in went unrecorded in *Wisden* though the popular newspapers gave it full coverage. It happened on the Monday of the Lord's Test between England and the West Indies in 1976. Again the batsman was Tony Greig and the bowler was Mike Holding, the West Indian who I bracket with Jeff Thomson as the world's fastest bowler. Possibly now that Thomson's pace has dropped, following his shoulder injury, Holding is *the* fastest in the world.

Greig had just struck Holding wide of mid on for four. The next ball appeared to be heading for Greig's head when he ducked under it with a fraction of a second to spare. Watching from square leg, it was impossible to tell whether it was deliberate but Greig obviously thought so. He glared down the pitch and Holding glared back. I did not hear any remarks exchanged although at his Press conference later, Greig was supposed to have said, 'I said a few things to him, the sort of things you would expect after being put in that position.'

Greig went on, 'I couldn't say whether it was the most dangerous ball I have ever faced because I didn't see it. I just closed my eyes and ducked. We have had a few of these deliveries bowled by the West Indies so far and I hope for the game's sake that it doesn't degenerate into a situation where beamers become acceptable.

'Anyone can bowl beamers. Now and again they can happen by mistake but the situation can arise where people start retaliating. Things could get nasty and that can't be allowed to happen. As far as I am concerned, beamers are totally unacceptable in any class of cricket.'

Five years earlier, Greig himself injured the Australian Graeme Watson, when an accidental full toss from him hit

Watson in the head. Watson was rushed to hospital and needed twenty-nine blood transfusions before he was removed from the critical list.

During that interview, Greig claimed the West Indies had bowled fifteen beamers in the series up to then. I had stood in all nine days' play and I didn't see fifteen beamers. It was a ridiculous claim. The only head-high full toss I remembered was the one delivered by Holding and I did not think that was intentional.

The West Indies denied next day that it was meant as a beamer. Clive Lloyd told the Press, 'Mike was trying to bowl a bit quicker and the ball just passed waist high down the legside and went for a bye. It was so wide, wicket keeper Deryck Murray had a job to get it.

'Holding hasn't played much cricket of late and what with trying to bowl faster and the wetness of the ball caused by perspiration, it slipped a bit. You don't think I would let a bowler bowl a beamer. I didn't feel it was necessary to make an apology because the ball was wide and didn't hit Greig.'

At a meeting of the International Cricket Conference shortly afterwards, the cricketing nations reaffirmed that the beamer was an illegal delivery. I cannot remember an instance in my playing or umpiring career where a bowler deliberately and maliciously bowled a beamer at a fellow cricketer. But I have seen a number of beamers bowled, all accidentally.

On each occasion, the bowler apologized. It is easy for a bowler to lose control, especially when the ball is new and slippery.

6

Arthur Fagg's Walk Out

From an umpiring point of view, the Second Test between
England and the West Indies at Edgbaston between 9 and 14
August 1973 was one of the most eventful Test matches ever
played in this country. For the first time in the history of Test
cricket an umpire said he was packing up and going home in the
middle of a Test.

Arthur Fagg was so incensed about the behaviour of the West
Indies captain Rohan Kanhai that he refused to take his position on the third morning of the match. It was a nerve-wracking
occasion for me. Only a month before, I made my début as a
Test umpire in the England v. New Zealand match at Headingley, at the comparatively young age of thirty-nine. I'd had only
two years on the list.

Now I was faced with the responsibility of being the senior
umpire in only my second Test. It was only a three-match series
and the West Indies won the first by 158 runs, their first victory
over England since 1966. They only had to draw the Second
Test to make sure of the rubber. Unless the pitch is rain-
affected and the conditions are right, it is not too difficult to
draw a game at Edgbaston.

The West Indies went slowly from the start. Their opener,
Roy Fredericks, batted throughout the opening day for his
98 not out in the West Indies total of 190–5. Ray Illingworth
bowled so accurately that he conceded only 18 runs in 27 overs,
18 of which were maidens. Next day the West Indies were all
out 327, Fredericks 150, Julien 54.

Boycott and Amiss opened confidently and were still together on 96 at the close. But early in Boycott's innings, he played forward against Keith Boyce, whose bowling was less hostile than usual because he was suffering from a bruised heel, and there was a loud appeal for a catch by wicket keeper Deryck Murray. Several other fielders joined in the appeal, including Kanhai, who was at slip. Arthur Fagg said 'Not out'.

I would never comment on a colleague's decision. Only Arthur was in a position to tell whether he thought Boycott was out or not. Kanhai took the decision badly, raising his arms like a footballer about to take a throw and then motioning them towards the ground in a gesture of annoyance. He also appeared to turn his back on the umpire. I couldn't tell from my position at square leg, but apparently some remarks were made later in the session.

I could see Arthur was still very upset when we came in at the end of the day's play. There are times when you feel like this in umpiring but I have found it is a mistake to worry about them. You simply have to get on with the job. As we sat there, him brooding and me fussing about, I said, 'Look, Arthur, I know you've had far more experience than I have but try not to worry about it.' He made no reply. He packed his bag and left.

Outside, two cricket reporters, Chris Lander of the *Daily Mirror* and Ian Todd of *The Sun*, approached him and asked him about the Kanhai incident. He told them all about it and about his feelings. Next morning at breakfast I was astounded at the headline, 'Test umpire in I'll Quit Threat'.

'I will ask Rohan Kanhai this morning whether he wants me to continue umpiring in this Test,' he was quoted. 'If not, I'll pack up and they can get someone else. If they won't accept decisions, there is no point carrying on. Why should I? I am nearly sixty. I don't have to live with this kind of pressure.

'I've had to live with it for two and a half hours out there. People don't realize how bad it has become. I don't enjoy umpiring Tests any more, nor Sunday League matches. There is so much at stake.

'The players shout for things and when they don't get the

decision, they react the way Kanhai reacted today. The game has changed, and not for the better. Umpires are under terrific pressure.

'The players have to learn to accept decisions, otherwise there is no point continuing. We are human, the same as everyone else, and we make mistakes, as players make mistakes. It doesn't matter whether it was out or not, it is the umpire's decision.

'Boycott signalled with his arm that the ball brushed his leg and looked at me for the decision. When players are trying it on, they don't look at you. I did not see any deviation.'

It was clear that Arthur had taken it very badly and was in an emotional state. He was one of England's leading umpires at the time. He'd helped me so much in my umpiring career that now I wanted to help him.

Outside the pavilion, TV men and Pressmen were milling around when I arrived some two and a half hours before the start of play. Arthur was putting all his remaining gear into his case. 'What are you doing, Arthur?' I said.

'I'm going home,' he said. 'I am not taking any further part in this match.' He offered his hand and wished me good luck. I asked him why he was going.

'Because of that incident yesterday,' he said. 'I am hoping I shall get an apology from Kanhai. If I don't that's it. I'm off home.'

There were continual knocks at the door as selectors, officials of the Warwickshire County Cricket Club and TV men kept coming in to ask what was happening.

Arthur kept repeating himself. 'I'm going home and I am not taking any further part in the match,' he said. The ground was filling up fast. Half an hour to go before the start, Arthur was still there and officials were unsuccessfully trying to persuade him to change his mind. I thought to myself, 'I wonder who is going to take over? I can't do it on my own.'

A Lord's official had rung Charlie Elliott at Leyton and Charlie was preparing to come. But it would take him at least three hours. Esmond Kentish, the manager of the West Indies side, was brought into the talks. There was no sign of an apology from the West Indies camp at that stage. Apparently they didn't think there was anything to apologize about.

I saw Leslie Deakins, secretary of the Warwickshire County Cricket Club and one of cricket's finest-ever administrators, and asked him who was going to stand at square leg. I would take the bowler's end but we'd need another umpire at square leg. Leslie had already discussed this with Alec Bedser, chairman of the selectors.

They both thought Alan Oakman, the former Sussex and England batsman who was the Warwickshire coach, would be the ideal man. Oakman had been on the umpire's list for a time, but Alan wasn't keen. 'There's no-one else,' he was told. Finally he agreed. The first bell went at 11.15 a.m. There had been no time for me to build myself up and prepare as I normally did. Arthur was still in the room.

11.20 and only five minutes before the final bell: I made one last appeal to him. 'Arthur,' I said, 'you're a fine umpire and I respect you as a man, but you've got to come out.'

'I'm sorry, Dickie,' he replied. 'I am not going out.' I went to both dressing-rooms to tell Ray Illingworth and Rohan Kanhai that Alan Oakman would be standing in for Arthur but only as the square leg umpire. They both accepted the news without comment.

11.25. The final bell. I put my jacket on, looked up at Alan Oakman (he's nearly as tall as Tony Greig) and he nodded. There was no sign of Arthur. The spectators showed no surprise when we emerged from the pavilion. I think the crowd were expecting it after what they had read in the popular newspapers and heard on the radio.

We had walked to the middle when Alan discovered that he had left the bails behind. He turned back to get them. I don't know what the crowd thought of that! Another walk off! Alan rushed past the West Indians as they were coming out on to the field.

I took the first over, with Alan at square leg. As we changed over, I suddenly heard a roar from the crowd. Arthur Fagg was walking out to the middle. I learned afterwards that Bedser and Kentish had managed to make him change his mind. Oakman was relieved to be allowed to go in. Arthur didn't say a word. He took up his position and the game resumed as though nothing had happened. But he looked strained and tired.

As the morning dragged on, there were more controversial moments as Boyce, Holder and Julien all bowled bouncers and Boyce and Julien were guilty of running down the pitch. The over rate got slower and slower. It was a thoroughly unsatisfactory exhibition by the West Indies and Arthur and I met in the middle of the pitch just before lunch to talk about the situation and what we could do to alter it.

We agreed to call both captains into our room during the lunch interval. That conference, the first of its type that I can remember, worked. Kanhai was very amenable and showed that the point had got home to him by getting his bowlers to bowl twenty-four overs in the first hour after lunch. In the two hours before the break, they bowled only twenty-six.

Twelve of these overs were bowled by Lance Gibbs. Lance bowled the fastest over of his era, sometimes under two minutes. He liked bowling quick overs. Bastmen used to work out a policy of stopping him just to upset him.

Boycott, injured in a collision with Murray the night before, resumed his innings and Kanhai moved a fielder backward of square as though he was going to tempt him with a bouncer. Vanburn Holder bowled short and Boycott just stood there and let the ball hit him in the left arm. A huge lump, like a rotten egg, came up in a second or two and he had to retire hurt again.

England made 305 and, in their second innings, the West Indies quickened up as they made 302. Kanhai, still playing it hard, declined to declare and when the last wicket fell, England were left just under four hours to make 325. The match petered out in a draw with Amiss 86 not out on his own ground. As the players came off, Kanhai went up to Fagg and shook his hand. 'There's no hard feelings,' he said. 'We've forgotten about it now.' Later it was learned that Kentish had apologized. No disciplinary action was taken by the TCCB.

I got on well with Kanhai myself. I have always rated him

one of the best batsmen ever produced by the West Indies. Significantly, he retained the captaincy when England visited the Caribbean in 1973–4.

It had not been an easy match to umpire. Some of England's bowlers had also been guilty of running down the pitch. Tony Greig, like Julien in the West Indies attack, was given a final warning.

The point about it was that the West Indies had five left-handers in their side, Fredericks, Ron Headley, Clive Lloyd, Alvin Kallicharran and Gary Sobers, and by marking the pitch in the prohibited zone, Greig was giving Derek Underwood something to bowl at from the other end.

Julien, left arm over the wicket, was assisting Lance Gibbs' off-spin by creating a rough on the line of off stump in his follow-through. It is unusual for two bowlers to be given final warnings in the same match but it happened in that Test. It was an unusual Test all round!

7

Bomb Scare

Play has been stopped in cricket matches for all kinds of odd reasons. Once at the Oval we came off because a batsman complained about the sun reflecting off the Shell building about a mile away! But the most dramatic stopping of play in a Test came in 1973 at Lord's, the bomb scare Test against the West Indies.

The ground was full to capacity, with thousands sitting on the grass. This privilege had been extended despite the pitch invasions in the First Test at the Oval and there must have been around 28,000 at Lord's that day. Just after lunch, a warning was telephoned claiming that a bomb had been planted in the ground. An IRA bombing campaign was going on in London at the time. Not long before, a bomb went off in Oxford Street.

It appeared that this call was genuine. There were many more that summer which weren't and which were ignored. But the police advised that the ground would have to be cleared and at 2.40 in the afternoon Billy Griffith, then secretary of MCC, made the announcement, asking spectators to leave the ground slowly. Few people wanted to go home so they all came on to the playing area. Thousands of people were milling around and it was a most confusing situation.

I sat on the covers which had been wheeled out to protect the playing pitch, thinking that was the safest place. It was most unlikely that a bomb would be under the covers! West Indian supporters wearing colourful shirts and holding bottles, laughed and joked with me.

'Don't worry, Mr Dickie,' one said. 'The bomb's already gone off. It's under the England batsmen. We put it there.' England were in danger of following on against the West Indies' first innings total of 652–8. In fact, they did follow on and lost by an innings and 226 runs, the second biggest defeat ever suffered by an England side. The worst defeat was at Brisbane on the 1946–7 tour of Australia.

After half an hour, Mr Griffith came on the tannoy again and told us the police wanted both teams off the field. We were escorted off in small groups and the England players and the umpires went to a tent in the gardens behind the pavilion. The West Indians went back to their hotel. It was a very frightening, confusing position to be in. After a break of eighty-five minutes, during which time the police searched all the buildings and the stands, it was announced that play could resume immediately. There had been no bomb after all, but the authorities couldn't take any chances.

That was the Test when Gary Sobers made 150 not out, one of his best innings. He was surely the greatest cricketer who ever lived, three cricketers rolled into one. Ray Illingworth lost his job as England captain after that game. Perhaps at forty-one he was considered too old.

He had the bad luck to come up against one of the most out-standing teams ever to come to England. Kanhai's side was full of all-rounders, Sobers the best of all, with Bernard Julien, Keith Boyce, Maurice Foster and Clive Lloyd. If it had a weakness it was in not finding a regular opening partner for Roy Fredericks. Steve Camacho, who probably would have had the job, went home after being struck in the face by Andy Roberts when playing for the tourists against Hampshire. Ron Headley was called up from Worcester but Deryck Murray took over after Headley scored only 1 and 11 in the Edgbaston Test.

Perhaps they should have tried Sobers there! Gary was one of my favourite cricketers. I can never remember him saying anything nasty on the field, or showing any anger. He was a thorough sportsman and socially he was a generous host. Once he invited me to his birthday party at his home near Nottingham when he was playing at Trent Bridge. His wife Pru, an Australian, was the perfect hostess.

On 2 June 1975, in the middle of one of the hottest summers on record, a most peculiar message came over the Press Association tapes in the newspaper, radio and TV offices. It said, '12.33 Buxton, snowing. A layer of snow covers the pitch.'

No-one could remember snow stopping play before. I was one of the umpires and when we inspected the pitch with some of the players, the snow was so deep that it was possible to bury your shoe in it. Clive Lloyd said he had never seen snow before. Buxton is one of England's highest grounds, but it was still unbelievable that it should be snowing in the middle of June.

Lancashire made 477–5, a record for the newly introduced 100-over regulation, with Lloyd hitting 167 and Hayes 104. There were 11 sixes and 60 fours in the Lancashire innings. 'Dusty' Rhodes and I grew tired of signalling the boundaries.

After the snow, the pitch became a pig of a wicket, one of the worst I've ever seen with the ball rearing head high off a length, and Derbyshire were bowled out twice in three and a half hours for 42 and 87 (87 is the bad luck number in Australian cricket). In the first innings, Ashley Harvey-Walker, the Derbyshire batsman, said, 'Here, take hold of these will you?' He handed me his false teeth! But I didn't need to have them in my pocket long. He was soon out, one of a number of batsmen who were terrified of being hit.

Batting on bad wickets is an art. It is a test of technique which few players pass successfully. Among the best bad wicket players of my time I would put John Edrich, Brian Close, Colin Cowdrey and Len Hutton. Once a player gets into a Test side and proves he has the temperament for Test cricket, scoring runs is not too difficult. The pitches are usually excellent and the batsman has plenty of time to build an innings.

But playing on bad pitches is another ball game, as Don Bradman found out on the infrequent occasions he had to perform on rain-affected pitches. It is also an art to be able to bowl well on bad pitches. The bowler has to bowl line and length and not be a fraction out otherwise the ball can shoot off to the boundary for byes or leg byes. If it is a stopping pitch, the good player will pull or cut the ball that is pitched too short. The best bad wicket bowlers of my time have been Derek Underwood, Ray Illingworth, Johnny Wardle, Tony Lock, Alec Bedser and Jim Laker, all great bowlers.

The incident with the sun shining off the Shell building happened in the 1974 Test between England and Pakistan at the Oval. Chris Old was the batsman and it was brilliantly sunny at the time, 6.15 in the evening. Old complained that he was being blinded by the sun being reflected off the Shell building. Intikhab, the Pakistan captain, stood where Old had been taking guard and had to admit that he was right. So off we went and the secretary explained the reason over the public address system. I couldn't remember sun stopping play before!

In another odd incident stopping play, again at the Oval, two spectators came on during a quiet period in the England *v.* Australia Test in 1975. One lowered his trousers and I thought it was going to be another streak, but he was wearing a pair of bathing trunks underneath.

He stood like a batsman just off the playing pitch while his mate went up to the other end and bowled a cheese roll. I thought the bowler, a chap named Bill Scrutton, had quite a fair action. Afterwards he told newsmen, 'It was a joke. The game needed livening up.' Asked if his 'delivery' turned as it pitched, he said, 'The cheese turned but the roll went straight on.'

No umpire likes interruptions from spectators. They can be very tiresome. But I thought that one had some style about it and made people laugh. The cricket was rather grim at the time. These diversions are perhaps more excusable if they are original but repetition is extremely tedious. Unless there are police right round the boundary, an impossible measure to bring about, or there is fencing, you can't stop people coming on.

The classic streak was at Lord's that same year, England *v.* Australia, 1975. The temperature was ninety-three degrees, the hottest day since 1948, when twenty-four-year-old Michael

Angelow, a ship's clerk from St Albans, ran on starkers and vaulted over the stumps. The picture of him jumping the wicket made the front pages of all the popular papers. TV producer David Kenning said, 'I cut to a long shot to avoid any embarrassment.' Next day Angelow was fined the same amount he won for his dare, £20, for 'outraging public decency'. His mother said, 'I could see it was him on TV. I'll smack his behind when he gets home.'

The worst light I have ever seen cricket played in was at Old Trafford in the Lancashire v. Gloucester Gillette Cup semi-final which I shall mention elsewhere. When Lancashire looked like losing, their captain Jackie Bond said to me, 'No point coming off now. It's impossible for us to win. We don't want to come back tomorrow.' Lancashire, of course, went on to win when David Hughes hit John Mortimore for 24 runs in an over. I was surprised that Morty kept bowling off stump and outside. He should have darted it in at his leg stumps. Hughes wouldn't have been able to hit those for six!

The only time I have had to miss time in the middle was at the Edgbaston Test in 1975. As we came off on the Saturday night, I felt a sharp pain in my back. I felt paralysed. Bernie Thomas, the Warwickshire and England physiotherapist, gave me an injection but it made no difference. I was unable to resume on the Monday morning and Tommy Spencer was called in.

Possibly I have back trouble because of the way I stand hunched over the stumps. But I always have had a stoop. My parents and school teachers were always telling me to stand up straight when I was a boy. Since that Edgbaston incident I sleep on a hard board, or if the hotel where I am staying doesn't have one, I drag the mattress off and sleep on it on the floor.

I have a brace which I wear when I drive. Doctors tell me that driving is one of the worst possible activities for anyone suffering from back trouble so I try to support my back as much as possible when I drive long distances. In the summer, I am rarely out of my car.

Cricket is held up for numerous reasons, many of them very

funny. Once in a Hampshire *v.* Yorkshire game at Bournemouth I was batting with Ray Illingworth when I thought I heard the sound of a race commentary. Closer inspection revealed that Colin Ingleby-Mackenzie, the Hampshire captain and a horse-racing nut, had a transistor in his pocket at mid off and was listening to the three o'clock from Newmarket. No-one complained about it.

In a match at Old Trafford once, between Lancashire and Middlesex, I stopped play when a Boeing 707 flew over so low that we couldn't hear ourselves speak. We sat down for half a minute, a well-earned respite.

Sometimes there is a short break while players chat to each other. There was an occasion when Richard Hutton, the very droll and witty son of Sir Len, was bowling to Kent's Graham Johnson, who kept playing and missing.

Hutton said, 'Excuse me, young man, what are you in the side for, can you bowl?'

Johnson replied, 'Not really.'

Hutton: 'Are you in for your fielding?'

Johnson: 'Not really.'

Hutton: 'Well, you can't bloody well bat.'

8

World Cup, 1975

The scenes at the end of the first-ever World Cup competition in 1975 were the most amazing I have ever experienced. It was bedlam. Before the last wicket fell in the Australia *v.* West Indies final, the crowd had invaded the field at Lord's and I was swamped in the rush. I was knocked on the head, no doubt accidentally, and was left dazed.

When the spectators were cleared, I found they'd frisked me of everything except the clothes I was wearing. Jeff Thomson's sweater which I had round my waist was gone. So were the spare balls, the spare bail and my white cap. At the presentation afterwards, Prince Philip said, 'Are you all right? I notice they've pinched your white cap.' I replied, 'Yes, sir, that's another one gone.'

He asked me when I had arrived in the morning at the ground. I said 8.30 a.m. It was now 8.50 p.m. 'That's a very long day for you,' said Prince Philip. A long day, but the peak day in my cricketing career. Australia *v.* West Indies was the greatest game of cricket I had ever seen. I felt privileged to have played a part in it.

The fact that it was such a long day and we were able to complete the match showed the advantage of playing the World Cup in England. It gets dark in most of the other cricketing countries early in the evening and none of them would be able to stage an event of this nature. Also, there was the added advantage of having many of the world's best players already in England taking part in county cricket in easily accessible parts of the country. I don't know whose idea it was but it was a brilliant conception. A total of 158,000 spectators paid £200,000 to watch the fifteen matches. The final, watched by 26,000 people, grossed a record £66,000 at Lord's. The profits were shared among the competing countries. The difference between cricket finances and soccer finances is still immense, for the takings of the England v. Italy World Cup game at Wembley in November 1977 came to £440,000, or more than twice as much for a single match as was taken in the whole of cricket's World Cup.

I knew I would be on the World Cup panel when I received a letter from Donald Carr in the winter. Eight umpires were invited. My first game was New Zealand v. East Africa at Edgbaston on 7 June. The East Africans, mainly of Indian descent from Kenya, were outclassed. Their captain, Harilal Shah, was a charming man and it was a pleasure to deal with him. He got a duck in that match, and in the next game too.

Glenn Turner, the New Zealand captain, made 171 not out which were more runs than the whole East African side achieved. They made just 128–8 off 60 overs. Hedley Howarth, a left-arm bowler of real Test class, was simply too good for them and they were just as badly beaten in my next game, against the Indians at Headingley. The crowd at Headingley was 720, some contrast from Lord's.

There was a funny moment when Farokh Engineer dropped a catch off Abid Ali and, though it didn't matter, the two men jabbered away angrily at each other in Urdu. Engineer, 54 not out, and Gavaskar, 65 not out, bettered the East Africa total in 29.5 overs. The real action that day, 11 June, was at Edgbaston, where a last wicket stand of 64 between Deryck Murray and Andy Roberts enabled the West Indies to beat Pakistan off the fourth ball of the last over. The West Indies, because of their pace bowling resources and depth in fast-scoring batsmen, were the favourites to lift the World Cup but there wasn't much to choose between them and Pakistan and the Australians. These three countries had the monopoly of the best players.

West Indies *v.* Australia at the Oval on 14 June was my next game. It was a preview of the likely final if both sides won their semi-finals the following Wednesday. When I arrived in the vicinity of the Oval at 8.30 a.m. it was impossible to move freely. The pavements were packed, mainly with West Indians. Spivs were selling tickets and people were trying to scale the walls.

Some of those who had got in had withheld the counterfoils of their ticket and were lobbing them back over the wall in tin cans to their friends outside! Long before the start, the ground was full and I bet many of them hadn't paid.

Clive Lloyd won the toss and asked the Australians to bat, not because it was a cloudy morning but because, like Ian Chappell the Australian captain, he liked chasing a total. The West Indians and Australians used this tactic throughout. Personally, I believe in batting first unless there is some help for your bowlers in the pitch or in the atmosphere. There has to be a good reason to insert and it is so easy to come unstuck, as Mike Denness discovered in the Edgbaston Test that year. His decision to put Australia in probably cost him the captaincy.

Lloyd's decision appeared to be justified early on. Bernard Julien had Rick McCosker caught by Roy Fredericks at short leg off his glove and I gave Alan Turner out lbw when Andy Roberts trapped him on the back foot. The impact of the blow made him wince. Roberts was bowling very fast that day. There had been a big build up about the fast bowlers in the Press and I think he wanted to show he was as quick as Lillee and Thomson. He was urged on by thousands of excited fans. There were banners everywhere. One said, 'Roberts, faster than any kangaroo.'

It is hard to judge pace from such close range but my impression was that Thomson was marginally faster than Andy when he bowled later in the day. But it was Keith Boyce, of slightly lesser pace, who struck the decisive blows in the morning, dismissing both Chappells in the space of six deliveries. The noise from the West Indians in the crowd was so loud that it was extremely difficult for David Constant and myself to hear the

nicks. Drums, trumpets, whistles and coke and beer tins full of
marbles were sounding off continuously.

Doug Walters, the next batsman in, had just heard that day
that he was receiving the MBE from the Queen for his services
to cricket but he had no time to celebrate in the middle. Walters
was run out for 7 by an extraordinary piece of out fielding by
Gordon Greenidge. Normally a slip fielder, Greenidge swooped
and threw the wicket down from almost sideways on. I was at that
end and it was just about the quickest I had ever moved to get
into position. Australia, 61–5, were in big trouble.

Ross Edwards made 58 before Viv Richards bowled him
with an off-break and Rod Marsh scored 52, but the total of
192 off 53.4 overs wasn't enough. The Australians had 38 balls
left. They hadn't paced their innings too well. The Edwards–
Marsh stand put on 99 for the 6th wicket and Edwards was
bowled after hitting successive fours off Richards. It had been
an intelligent move to put Richards on to bowl. I don't know
why more spin bowlers aren't used in one-day cricket.

Dennis Lillee, opening the bowling for the Australians, let
two bouncers go in his first over and I said, 'Now come on,
Dennis, you know the position about bouncers in these matches.'
He said, 'All right,' and didn't bowl another bouncer in the
match. The International Cricket Conference were concerned
not only that the bouncer would be used as an intimidatory
weapon but as a delivery which batsmen couldn't score from if
it was too high.

Greenidge was lbw to Walker for 16 but Fredericks 58 and
Kallicharran 78 soon had the match won for the West Indies.
Kalli was simply magnificent, hooking and cutting Lillee with
ferocity and bringing the West Indian supporters to their feet,
those who weren't already standing. Lillee made the mistake of
bowling too short on a slow, easy-paced wicket. He tried to rib
Kalli but it didn't work and when Kalli reached his fifty, he was
the first to go up to him and shake his hand. Lillee is like that: a
tough opponent but a generous one when he has been bettered
on the day.

In one sequence, Kalli scored 35 off 10 deliveries from Lillee –

4, 4, 4, 4, 4, 1, 4, 6, 0, 4. Before being caught by Ashley Mallett
off Lillee, he hit a six and thirteen fours. Lillee's figures were
10–0–66–1. The West Indies won by seven wickets with 14
overs remaining.

In the scramble at the end, I had yet another white cap stolen
and there was an amusing sequel. A few days later I was travelling on a bus in London and the West Indian conductor was
wearing a cap which looked like one of mine.

I said to him, 'Where did you get that cap from?'

'It was from Dickie Bird, the Test umpire,' he said proudly. He
didn't recognize me and I decided against trying to reclaim it!

I had a day off when the semi-finals were played so I went to
Headingley to watch England take on Australia. There was
plenty of low cloud about, conditions which help swing bowling.
When it is fine and sunny at Headingley, the ball never does
anything. But in cloudy conditions, it is liable to swing unpre-
dictably. Ian Chappell won the toss and put England in.

Both sides left out spinners to accommodate the extra seamer.
Australia's Gary Gilmour came in for Ashley Mallett. That was
a match-winning move because Gilmour skimmed England out
for 93 in 26.2 overs with figures of 12–6–14–6. Not only did he
swing it in the air, he moved it off the pitch too. I met Len
Hutton and he thought the England batsmen had made it
worse for themselves by playing back. 'They should be on the
front foot,' he said. 'The fellow is bowling a full length.'

Some of the England batsmen blamed the sightscreen at the
Football end. They said it was difficult to pick the ball up. The
Australian batsmen had difficulty too and were 39–6 at one
stage before Gilmour came in and hit 28 to win the match.

I called him Gary Glitter, but to his team mates he was 'Gus'.
He's a fine cricketer and I think he was badly missed on the
1977 tour of England. The previous season in Australia he
played with a chipped bone in the foot and kept quiet about it.
But for that, he would have been back in England for a second
tour.

Mike Denness was upset about the pitch. It was the same one
that had been used for the Australia *v.* Pakistan match ten days

earlier. Denness claimed the bounce was uneven and several of his batsmen were lbw when the ball squatted. George Cawthray, the Headingley groundsman, told the Press, 'It would have been the same if they'd played on another pitch. It was the atmosphere that did it, not the pitch.'

In the other semi-final the West Indies defeated New Zealand by five wickets, so the stage was set for a final between the best two sides in the competition, Australia and the West Indies. Tommy Spencer was my fellow umpire at Lord's. Once again the weather was fine and sunny. The atmosphere at Lord's resembled what it had been at the Oval when the two teams last met. Chappell won the toss and inserted, his customary procedure.

Dennis Lillee opened from my end. The rest of us were pretty tense but Dennis was cracking jokes and laughing. He relished the occasion. When Fredericks was 7 he hooked one of Lillee's short deliveries splendidly for what would have been a colossal six into the pavilion.

Lillee stood in the middle of the pitch applauding. 'What a magnificent shot,' he said. 'He's out,' I said. Lillee hadn't seen that Fredericks had trodden on his leg stump. Fredericks was wearing rubber soles, not spikes. With an early start and the possibility of some dew still remaining, that was a tragic mistake.

Gilmour opened from Tommy Spencer's end. Chappell probably wanted to exploit Gilmour's success at Headingley. Also, he may have thought that Jeff Thomson might have let slip a few bad balls with the new ball when it was shiny. Thomson has a habit of doing that. Sometimes his first over with the new ball can be erratic and expensive. But Gilmour wasn't very tight in his first over. He was no-balled three times for overstepping.

The Australians had another wicket down at 27 when Kallicharran, who'd virtually won the match for the West Indies at the Oval, was caught Marsh off Gilmour. Kalli was trying to cut and his feet weren't in the right position. It was riveting cricket. Gordon Greenidge, normally so free at Lord's, was pinned down, eventually being dismissed by Marsh at 50–3. Kanhai blocked away at one end while the new batsman, Clive Lloyd, played the way he knows best. If Lloyd had gone early that might have been it. But he played the greatest innings I have seen in my thirty years in the game.

Lillee was brought back into the attack to test him. Because Clive tends to blink away behind those thick glasses, opposing captains feel his eyesight isn't so good and he can't pick up fast bowling. Lillee bowled short and Clive pulled him square for six: the shot of the series.

When he was 26, Clive gave an extremely difficult chance to Ross Edwards. Edwards dived but couldn't hold it. That was another turning point because Lloyd and Kanhai added 149 for the 4th wicket in thirty-six overs, a record. Lloyd's 100 came off 82 balls. Two runs later he chased a wide delivery from Gilmour outside the leg and got an edge trying to glance. Marsh caught it and threw it up.

There was plenty of noise from the crowd but I heard the snick and saw the deviation. But I wasn't sure that it carried to Marsh. It is a curiosity at Lord's that sometimes from the Nursery end it is impossible to see low catches behind the wicket because there is a slight dip at the other end. Kanhai said, 'That didn't look as though it carried.'

Lloyd, who very rarely walks, stood his ground. There was a tremendous hubbub. The Australians in the crowd, and there were thousands, were shouting for Lloyd to be given out. The West Indians wanted him kept in. The neutrals wanted him to stay too, I imagined. I walked towards Tommy Spencer to ask if the catch was up. He said it was. I raised the finger. There was no doubt about the ball being hit but I had to clear up the other point.

It is not often that I make a point of seeing the TV playbacks but I did that night. The film showed that the catch was a fair one. The crowd must have wondered what all the fuss was about. But I knew I was right to consult Tommy Spencer. Rohan Kanhai had the same misgivings as I had. Only those of us at that end could have been deceived.

The West Indies total of 291–8 off their allotted sixty overs was an immense target to reach. Gillette Cup sides rarely achieve it. Here the Australians were facing the tension of the world's biggest one-day match as well as world-class fast bowling. The odds were heavily against them but many people, including the Australians themselves, thought they would have pulled it off but for five run outs. When you look at it, that is an incredible number of self-inflicted dismissals.

McCosker went early and Alan Turner was run out at 81 by a brilliant underarm throw from Viv Richards. The two Chappells took the score to 115 when Greg was run out, again by Richards. Ian hit the ball square between Julien and Richards, shouting 'yes' as he hit it. But Greg said 'no' and Ian stopped a couple of yards down the wicket. Julien swooped, but missed the ball. Greg then said 'yes' and set off. By then Richards had the ball in his hand and Ian, realizing there was no point in sending him back, went off down the wicket. Richards threw at the only stump he could see and miraculously hit it. Greg was well out.

Doug Walters added 47 with Ian Chappell before Chappell went to Viv's hat-trick piece of fielding. Ian played wide of mid on, began to run, waited as Richards appeared to miss it and then started to run again. Richards threw in and Clive Lloyd, who was bowling, whipped the bails off. Viv Richards had only scored 5 but he'd almost won the match with his fielding.

Lloyd's bowling, often used by Lancashire in one-day matches, also played a part because Clive only conceded 38 runs in his twelve overs which made him more economical than Andy Roberts (45), Bernard Julien (58), Boyce (54) and Holder (65). When Ross Edwards and Gary Gilmour went, both victims of Keith Boyce, the Australians seemed resigned to defeat.

But when last man Dennis Lillee joined Jeff Thomson at 233–9, Lillee said jauntily, 'We'll get these, Dickie.' Fifty-nine runs were needed. I couldn't see it myself. But slowly the runs started coming and the crowd became more and more excited.

Thomson skied a ball to Fredericks at mid off and was caught.

Captain of Raley Schools
First Team. Winners of
Barnsley and District Schools
Trophy, 1948.

On the way to my highest
score, 181 not out. Yorkshire *v.*
Glamorgan at Bradford, 1959.
I was dropped next match!

Celebrating the winning of the
championship by Yorkshire in 195[...]
with Phil Sharpe, Don Wilson an[...]
Jackie Birkenshaw.

Opening the batting for Yorkshire [...]
MCC with Vic Wilson at Scarborou[...]
Wilson replaced me in the next m[...]
but he didn't get any runs in this [...]

Yorkshire's 1960 championship side. *Left to right:* Cyril Turner (scorer), Brian Bolus, Doug Padgett, Don Wilson, Bob Platt, Mel Ryan, Dickie Bird, Jackie Birkenshaw, Phil Sharpe, George Allcock (masseur). *Middle row:* Ray Illingworth, Brian Close, Vic Wilson, Fred Trueman, Jimmy Binks. *Front row:* Ken Taylor, Bryan Stott.

H. D. Bird bowled Sobers, Grace Road, Leicester, 1963. Feet all screwed up as the ball swings to remove middle stump.

ABOVE LEFT My first Test match a
an umpire: England *v.* New Zealan
at Headingley, 1973. Home territor

ABOVE RIGHT How Roy Ullyett
saw me.

World Cup Final medal, 1975.
Solid silver and rather weighty!

Talking to the fans when the bomb scare interrupted play in England *v*. West Indies Test at Lord's in 1973. Somewhere near those covers is the pitch.

Snow stopped play at Buxton, 1975. *Left to right:* Peter Lever, Clive Lloyd, Frank Hayes, Dickie Bird and David Lloyd, of Lancashire.

Fifth Test, England *v.* West Indies, 1976. Umpire Spencer and I bring the players off after West Indian supporters invade the pitch after Mike Holding bowls Tony Greig.

A spectator thinks the game needs livening up. England *v.* Australia at the Oval, 1975.

Barnsley Cricket Club with the Rt. Hon. Roy Mason, Secretary of State
for Northern Ireland, the most protected man in the United Kingdom.
Barnsley born and bred, like the author.

Shaking hands with HM the Queen during the Trent Bridge match, England
v. Australia, in her Jubilee Year.

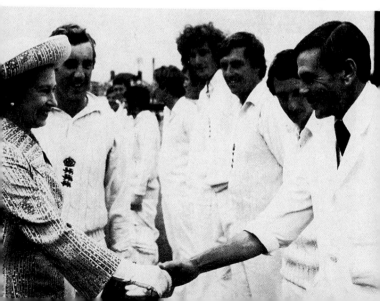

Three Yorkshiremen – Geoff Boycott, Sir Harold Wilson and myself – at a dinner to celebrate Boycott's hundredth first-class century, in Leeds, 1977.

Ronnie Jukes presenting me with the 'Yorkshire Personality of the Year Award', 1977.

But it was a no-ball. The crowd, thinking the match was over, ran on in their hundreds. I was engulfed. My white cap went, Thomson's sweater, the spare ball and I felt a sharp blow on the head which left me dizzy. I could just hear Lillee shouting, 'Come on, we can run 17 off this and win the game.' He was running up and down.

Thomson was less enthusiastic. 'Don't be stupid,' he screamed. 'One of these so and so's could have the ball in his pocket.' Police were on the pitch trying to restore order. The fans were asked to go back to their seats because the match wasn't over. Reluctantly, they began to drift away.

Tommy Spencer came over. 'What the bloody hell is going on?' he said. 'How many did they run?' I said I didn't see what had happened to the ball. It had been swallowed up in the crowd though later it was thrown back. We decided to give the batting side 4 runs because Fredericks' overthrow had been stopped by a spectator.

The game restarted but at 274, with 18 still needed off eight deliveries, Thomson was finally run out and the West Indies won. On came the crowd again like Genghis Khan and his army. I was surrounded by milling West Indians. Keith Boyce was yanked over and as he lay on the ground, fans took off his boots and made off with them as souvenirs. They stripped Thomson of his pads, his bat and his gloves. Police helmets were everywhere.

As we scrambled off, I said to Lillee, 'How many did you run?' He said, 'Seventeen.' It was the greatest day of my life. Fifty-seven per cent of the population was watching on TV. I hope the next World Cup, in 1979, is as successful.

My reward was a fee of £100 and a large silver medal presented by Prince Philip. But I didn't worry about the size of the cheque. I would have done it for nothing. The honour of being selected to umpire this great match was enough.

Prince Philip congratulated us on the way we handled the game. So did the Australians. Three days later I received a letter from Fred Bennett, the Australian manager, which read, 'Dear Dickie, This is just a brief note to say on behalf of Ian, myself and the team, how much we appreciated your efforts last Saturday in the World Cup Final at Lord's.

'It was a long day for everyone, certainly it must have been a trying day for you with the crowd problems. The job you did was much appreciated by all of us. I hope you have now recovered from your injury and look forward to seeing you again soon. Kind regards.' Colin Cowdrey also sent a card: 'Many congratulations on your superb handling of the various games in the World Cup. It contributed much to the success of the event. Nice that England have the best umpires in the world. Sincerely, Colin.'

It was a relief to be able to sit down and relax before going down to the West Indian dressing-room to join in the champagne celebrations. The West Indian players were 'jumping' in their jockstraps. The din was deafening.

9

The Australians

Dennis Lillee threw the ball at me. 'That ball's out of shape,' he said. I looked at it and said, 'It's all right. Keep on bowling, it will knock itself back into shape.'

'Well, I'm not going to finish the over so they'll not get a chance to knock it back into shape,' replied Dennis.

I was firm. 'I am not changing that ball,' I said. Lillee: 'But what are we going to do?' 'I am not budging,' I said. 'We might as well sit down.'

So in the middle of a session of the fourth day's play in the Fourth Test between England and Australia at the Oval in 1975, we all sat down. I don't know what the radio and TV commentators made of it, or the Press. There was no mention of a sit-down strike in the newspapers the next day.

The ball was in a bad way but I didn't propose to change it in the middle of an over. At that time the public were getting fed up with continual inspections of cricket balls. Hardly a ball seemed to last its allotted eighty-five overs. Dennis had been chipping away about this particular one for some time. He'd been toiling on a slow pitch against an England side who were merely intent on surviving.

Ian Chappell, the Australian captain, came up. 'What's all the trouble?' he said. I said, 'Ian, Dennis won't finish the over unless we change the ball and I told him to get on with it. We'll change it at the end of the over.'

Ian Chappell never likes to be called 'skipper' or 'captain', which is the usual style of address among English sides. If anyone called him 'skipper' he would reply, 'My name's Ian.'

'Come on, Dennis,' he said. 'Get on with your bloody bowling.' Lillee is an independent character but he wouldn't ignore an instruction from his captain.

'All right then,' he said. 'I'll finish the over but I'll bowl off-spinners.' He got up, walked back a few yards and came up and bowled the perfect off-break, on a length and turning just a little. His next three deliveries to finish the over were just the same.

'Now then, Dickie, what do you think of that then?' he said. I thought he had a career ahead of him as a spin bowler when he no longer wanted to bowl fast! He handed me the old ball. It was in a terrible shape and we replaced it. I hadn't changed it in the middle of the over because it sometimes happens that the ball does get knocked back into shape, particularly when a fast bowler is bowling.

As I produced the new ball (well not brand new, but a ball that had been used for a similar number of overs in the nets) Dennis said with a smile, 'Thanks very much, Dickie.'

I had never known a bowler refuse to carry on in a Test match before. I was asked what would have happened if Ian Chappell had supported Lillee. Would the Test match have been abandoned? My answer was I didn't think it would have come to that. Ian Chappell wouldn't want to throw all that hard work away. England saved the match by making 538 in their second innings in reply to Australia's 532-9 and Lillee took 4-91 off 52 overs.

It was a highly praiseworthy piece of bowling by Lillee. He received no encouragement from the pitch or the conditions but kept at it for more than two days. He is one of the few bowlers whose control is such that he can predict what he is going to bowl.

In that match he said, 'I am going to bowl an off cutter and it will rap him on the pads and I'll be up for an appeal, you watch!' He ran up, bowled . . . and it was an off cutter and it did hit the batsman on the pads. But I spoiled it for him by turning down the appeal. We had quite a chat. He is pretty talkative on the field.

Only one bowler in my experience had similar control: Alec Bedser, now chairman of the selectors. Alec could bowl any kind of delivery on request.

Dennis is very competitive and is usually having a mumble at the batsman, especially if the batsman is playing and missing. My policy is to keep at him when this happens, saying things like, 'Come on, Dennis, get on with your bowling.' He takes it well and we never had a cross word.

Once when a batsman edged the ball through the slips a couple of times, he said, 'This fellow has a better cutting edge than a Wilkinson Sword.'

Just as Bedser used to love bowling at Arthur Morris, the Australian opener on the 1948 tour of England, so Lillee delights in bowling at Dennis Amiss. When Amiss came in during one match, Lillee said, 'I can get this fellow out for a pastime, Dickie.' On another occasion, he said, 'I can get him out with a water melon.'

Lillee didn't bowl many bouncers during that 1975 tour. Before it began, the critics were anticipating a bouncer war but it never materialized. Jeff Thomson is not a frequent user of the bouncer. His most dangerous ball is the delivery just short of a length which gets up chest high. His action and extra pace seem to be able to produce this extremely effective ball on odd occasions. The batsman has to play it. He can't duck out of the way as he can with a bouncer.

I rank Dennis Lillee number one among the great fast bowlers I have seen. Mike Holding may be faster or straighter, but Lillee has more of the qualities you want from a fast bowler: hostility, variation, swing, a great bouncer and a competitive nature. Lillee has had to work exceptionally hard to get to the top. When his back went in the West Indies, he spent hours every day exercising to get himself back to peak fitness.

As for his behaviour on the field, all I can say is that it has never worried me. Dennis Lillee and the Australians play cricket the way we play it in Yorkshire; very hard and competitively and occasionally with some needle. Like the Yorkshireman, they play to win and don't like losing.

During the 1975 tour, an English cricket lover said to Chappell, 'You chaps are a very good team but you are a bunch of bastards on the field.' Chappell said that caused him satisfaction because he would much sooner lead a team like that than a team of nice guys. 'I believe that on the field the players should concentrate on giving their best to the team, to themselves and to winning,' he said. 'In other words, playing hard and fairly within the rules. To my mind, doing all that left no time for being a nice guy.'

I found that Chappell's behaviour on the field did not present any problems. If you were fair with him, he was fair with you. If you treated the Australians as human beings, they responded. If you talked their way, and treated them as professional cricketers, there was nothing to worry about.

Greg, Ian's brother, is much quieter and less demonstrative but he, too, is a fine captain. He never says much on the field. He is like a Guardsman, head upright, back straight – he'll never have back trouble! Being the outstanding batsman in the side meant he had the total support of all the players under him.

I saw him make two centuries in county matches and, particularly at Bath, he looked a good enough player to stand with any batsman in the world. In Tests, however, he wasn't so prolific. He never complained but I think he was weighed down by all kinds of worries – the Packer business and its effect on team spirit, the form of some of his younger players, criticism from the Australian Press and the soreness under the arches of his feet which left him less than 100 per cent fit after the Trent Bridge Test.

It was uncharacteristic of him when he dropped a couple of chances. I would rate him up with Ian, his brother, Bobby Simpson, Eddie Barlow and Philip Sharpe as one of the best catchers of post-war years. The Australian line-up in the slip cordons differs from England's though latterly England have copied it to some extent.

The Australian first slip stands much wider than the English first slip. This is because the Australians reckon the wicket keeper can catch anything within about six feet of his right hand. You never see Rod Marsh diving across first slip, whereas Alan Knott often does it. The Australian line is also straighter and when the fast bowlers like Jeff Thomson and Dennis Lillee are bowling, the line is stretched out in such a way that they can do without a third man.

The Australians stand fairly straight, with hands at hip level, which is not the way we teach in England. Probably this comes from playing on harder wickets where the ball bounces higher. But in England, coaches advise youngsters to get right down with hands close to the ground. It is easier to come up than it is to go down. Learie Constantine used to preach that and there was no better catcher than Learie.

The Australian slip ring is always chattering away. Their slip fielders are about the most talkative in world cricket but as soon as the bowler starts his run, they stop. I cannot remember an incident where a batsman has had to draw away because the slip fielders were talking in a Test match. By the 1977 series in England when the Ashes were regained, England's slip cordon became pretty talkative with Greig, Brearley and Knott around.

Six hours is a long time to be out in the middle and there is usually plenty to talk about, not all about the state of play either. There was the story that was told about Arthur Mitchell, the old Yorkshire coach, when Norman Yardley, just down from Cambridge University, was asked to field in the slips in a Yorkshire match. Yardley hadn't stood in the slips before and it was looked on as a privileged position. You had to serve an apprenticeship first before you qualified to stand as a Yorkshire slip fielder.

Arthur said to him, 'How's tha got here? I hope you've got some good stories to tell.'

The most talkative cricketer I think I have ever encountered is Derek Randall. He never stops. When the ball is hit towards him he says things like 'go on, try a run'. Some of the Australians found him a bit much even by their standards. Not all the

Australians are chatty though. Graham McKenzie, known as 'Garth' because of his immense strength, was about the only bowler I have come across who never appealed. Even when it was a plumb lbw he would still leave it to the wicket keeper. I can't ever remember him shouting for anything. I thought he would go on and beat Trueman's record number of Test wickets and was surprised when the Australians left him out. He was fit enough to carry on and he has proved that in the Packer matches.

Fast bowlers, it is said, go in pairs. The Australians have had three great partnerships this century in Syd Gregory and Ted McDonald, Ray Lindwall and Keith Miller and latterly Jeff Thomson and Dennis Lillee. But 'Garth' McKenzie was virtually on his own. He had no-one at the other end to soften batsmen up.

When he first came to England as a teenager in 1961 that outstanding left-arm bowler Alan Davidson was at the end of his eminent career, and in latter years McKenzie had a succession of what I would term phantom bowlers as his partner, bowlers like Laurie Mayne, Frank Misson, Grahame Corling, Dave Renneberg, Ron Gaunt and Alan Connolly. None of these was genuinely fast. The most effective partner he had was Neil Hawke, who was medium fast but swung the ball a fair bit. Neil liked England so much that he settled down here after his last tour and lives and works in the North of England. If McKenzie had operated with a Lillee or Thomson at the far end, I feel sure he would have broken all records.

People will always argue about the respective pace of bowlers. Is Thomson faster than Miller or Lindwall? Was Gregory faster than any of them? I saw Miller at Bradford in 1956 when I was Yorkshire's 12th man and he was no longer fast.

What I do remember of that day were the taunts of a Yorkshire wag who kept shouting insults at Miller in the field. When the players came in for lunch, Miller went straight over to the man, grabbed him by the collar and marched him off to the Australian dressing-room where he proceeded to lock him in the toilet. 'What are you going to do about that then?' he said.

Miller was an all-time great. He didn't care one iota about protocol or tradition.

In the umpiring world, it is said that you haven't umpired a Test match until you have done an England *v.* Australia Test and I agree with that. The atmosphere is much more electric. It is a 'real' Test.

Most Australians have a sense of humour on the field. Doug Walters would always be coming up to me and saying, 'Got a fag, Dickie?' He is a chain smoker and is reckoned to go through three or four packets a day. For all that, he is one of the quickest runners in the side and never seems out of breath.

He caused some consternation when the official team picture was taken once. It was an expensive job, well mounted and presented, but when the final prints came up, someone noticed a small object at the feet of Walters as he sat in the front row. It was a packet of his favourite cigarettes from the company which employed him. I gather it had to be painted out!

Rod Marsh was always chiding me. 'You want to drink a proper beer,' he said. 'An Australian Swan lager.' They had Swan or Fosters in their dressing-room but I preferred Guinness.

I was in the Australian dressing-room at the end of that Oval Test when Dennis Lillee came up and presented me with his official tour tie. With it was a note saying, 'Thanks for everything, from Dennis and the boys.' He had autographed it, 'Best wishes, Dennis Lillee.'

I was quite taken aback. It meant that Dennis had to fly off the next day with no tie because the players were only issued with one each. Now that tie of his has a special place in my display cabinet at my home. That gesture meant more to me than any amount of money. It showed I had the respect of some of the world's most competitive cricketers. I couldn't have wished for a higher recommendation.

Contrary to some people's impression, the Australians have always played cricket with humour as well as with aggression. Before I played with Leicestershire, they had two great characters from Australia on the staff, Jack Walsh, a slow left-hand Chinaman and googly bowler, and Vic Jackson, a batsman.

In one match Leicestershire were playing Lancashire at Grace Road and Cyril Washbrook was starting his innings for Lancashire.

Washbrook always said he could read Walsh's deliveries and predict which way they were going to turn. Walsh turned the ball considerably and there were many good players playing at the time who couldn't pick the googly from the Chinaman. Walsh bowled a Chinaman and Jackson, fielding at first slip, spotted it instantly and darted across to leg slip. Washbrook, lunging forward, got an edge and it went straight into Jackson's hands. 'I told you I could read him and you couldn't,' said Jackson.

10

'Who's Grovelling Now?'

The first time an invasion of the pitch caused a temporary halt in play in a Test match in this country was at the Oval in 1976 when we were off for thirteen minutes. Tony Greig had just played two fine cover drives for four with that extravagant shot of his when Mike Holding shattered his stumps with his blockhole ball.

Hundreds of West Indians rushed on to the pitch, mobbing Holding and jeering Greig as he departed. Bill Alley and I were powerless to do anything about it. One expensively dressed supporter reeled £50 in fivers off a thick wad of notes and, handing them to me, said, 'Give that to Holding for bowling Greig.' Holding, surrounded by well wishers, had refused to take the money so I took it to save any argument. I handed it to Holding later.

'Here,' said the man. 'Give this to Greig.' He handed me a 10p piece. Holding was hoisted into the air and for a minute or two it was like a Port of Spain Carnival out there in the middle. There was nothing for it but to take the players in. It was impossible to restart the match.

Bottles and litter covered the outfield and had to be cleared away. *Wisden* reported, 'Greig raised hopes of a long stay with two grand cover drives off Holding. But trying again he was bowled off his pads. A disgraceful scene followed. A huge section of the crowd, mainly West Indian, swept over the ground and trampled on the pitch with the departure of the England captain.'

I had never known cricketers and spectators react in such a way as the West Indians did that brilliant summer as Greig strode in on the nine occasions he came to the crease. The fans would start chanting and the West Indian bowlers would roll their sleeves up another knot and find a few more yards of pace from somewhere. I don't think the West Indies fast bowlers liked Tony Greig too much!

It went back to Greig's use of just one word in a 'Sportsnight' interview the night before the start of the First Test at Nottingham. The word was 'grovel'. The *Concise Oxford English Dictionary* defines it as 'lie prone, humble oneself (often in the dirt or dust), abject, low, base'.

I didn't hear the interview myself but reports of it made most of the popular newspapers the next morning. The *Daily Mirror* headlined it 'England skipper's amazing outburst against West Indies'.

What Greig said was, 'If the West Indies are on top, they are magnificent. If they are down, they grovel. And with the help of Brian Close and a few others, I intend to make them grovel.' That one remark must have added thousands to the attendances at the five Tests: nearly all the West Indians who could afford to go to Test cricket wanted to see him proved wrong.

Greig also criticized the West Indian batting. 'Alvin Kallicharran is very much out of form,' he said. 'He's probably batting as badly as he's ever done. I didn't realize until my Sussex lads took them on at Hove in our last match how out of touch the West Indian batsmen were. A player of Lawrence Rowe's ability – he scored 300 against us in Barbados two years ago – should be doing much better, even if he has had a spot of fitness trouble. And Roy Fredericks hasn't exactly been setting the green fields of England on fire, has he?

'I know these are big statements and I might be proved wrong but that's what I feel.'

I don't think Greig meant it in an insulting way. Most people said England had no chance against Clive Lloyd's side and Greig was merely trying to instil some confidence and wind his players up. I was sure it wasn't a racially inspired reference because Greig is not like that. But it was rather unfortunate that these words should be delivered by a man who was speaking in a South African accent, even if he was England's captain.

Next day Alec Bedser, chairman of the England selectors, defended Greig. 'It is totally unfair to take the word grovel out of context,' he said. 'What Greig means is that he is going to do his best to beat the West Indies. He has instilled the right attitude in the England side.'

Clyde Walcott, the West Indies manager, was philosophical. 'If Greig cares to make comments about us, then it is up to him,' he said. 'I am not concerned. This is just another of those psychological moves – don't call it a war – that go on before a big match.'

At his first press conference, Greig said he didn't regret his choice of words. He was to be asked that question many times during the series and he stuck to the same answer. Some West Indians brought out a record, 'Who's Grovelling Now', and there were Greig banners at all the grounds. I think the West Indian supporters really loved him. They responded to his gestures and it made the cricket more entertaining.

When the series was ending, Greig made a point of going over to the part of the Oval where the West Indian support was at its strongest, near the small scoreboard to the left of the pavilion, and getting down on his knees and grovelling. It was a marvellous moment and made a vivid picture for one of the popular newspapers.

They were one fan short there at the time because the one who had been shouting my name all day was no longer present. He was in hospital, I learned. He was sitting on top of the wall, drinking away throughout the day, when he suddenly toppled backwards and fell fifteen feet to the pathway below. I heard the 'ting-a-ling' of the ambulance that came to take him away.

The West Indies won that Test by 231 to clinch the series 3-0. Holding's 14–149 was the greatest exhibition of fast bowling I had ever seen. If it had been at Lord's, where conditions are more favourable to pace, it would have been understandable: but at the Oval, the graveyard of bowlers! He was so quick through the air, and so straight. Eleven of his fourteen victims were either bowled or lbw. The light was very good most of the time but he beat them through the air by sheer pace.

He is a nice, shy lad who doesn't say much in the middle. He told me he was a 400 metres champion back home in Jamaica and could have taken part in the Olympics but for putting cricket first. He certainly had the smoothest, most athletic approach to the wicket of any bowler I had ever seen.

Holding was the dominant bowler of the series and Viv Richards the dominant batsman. Viv made 291 in the West Indies first innings 687–8 declared, a monumental innings. He was bowled, playing on, by Greig. Like all the truly great players, Viv has so much time to play. He doesn't go to the ball. He lets it come to him and he hits it late. The bad, or average, player is the one who starts moving as the ball leaves the bowler's hand. He is putting himself in a position where he can't change. If he is starting to go forward, he can't go back when he realizes he has misjudged the length.

Geoff Boycott, Barry Richards, Clive Lloyd, Viv Richards, all these players move late. It is a sign of genuine class. Viv made 829 runs in the series for an average of 118·42 and but for missing the Lord's Test through illness, would probably have topped 1,000 runs.

England owed much to Dennis Amiss, who had been recalled after the failures of David Steele as an opener at Leeds. Without his 203 in the first innings, it would have been over at least a day earlier, and perhaps that fellow wouldn't have tumbled off that wall! Amiss had thought a vast amount about his vulnerability to pace and decided the answer was a new, opened-up stance. He looked awkward at the crease but managed to stick it out pluckily for hour after hour.

It proved his undoing in the end. By going across so far to make sure he was behind the line, he exposed his leg stump and Holding duly removed it, bowling him behind his legs.

Like Illingworth in 1973 it was Greig's bad luck to be leading England at a time when they were confronted by one of the strongest sides ever to tour England. Clive Lloyd's team was full of exciting stroke players like Richards, Gordon Greenidge, Roy Fredericks, Alvin Kallicharran, Lawrence Rowe, Lloyd himself and Collis King, and its complement of fast bowlers, Holding, Roberts, Daniel and Holder, has never been surpassed. Sir Don Bradman's 1948 side, often hailed as the greatest ever, only had two bowlers of great pace, Keith Miller and Ray Lindwall.

There was no respite for England's batsmen: they were facing frightening pace nearly all day and every day. Only in one department was Lloyd's team deficient: in spin bowling. They lacked a replacement for Lance Gibbs and they could have done with an Alf Valentine type of slow left-hand bowler.

England tried to counter the West Indies' advantage in playing strength by relying on experienced players. The surprise selection was Brian Close at the age of forty-five. When we were standing together at square leg in the West Indies first innings at Trent Bridge, he said, 'You know, lad, if I get a score here I'll play for England for the next five years. They'll never get me out.'

He made 2 in the first innings and 36 not out in the second and retained his place at Lord's where he batted with immense courage, scoring 60 and 46. He also battled it out stubbornly in the Old Trafford Test before he was dropped. Age was against him but his total of 166 runs in three Tests was only exceeded by David Steele, Tony Greig, Alan Knott and Bob Woolmer, all of whom played in five Tests. And he did come second in the averages behind the other veteran who was dropped, John Edrich.

Except for Headingley, when he returned to form with scores of 116 and 76 not out, Greig had a lean summer with the bat, seven times failing to get past 20. With the average Test cricketer, I reckon half of any success is down to temperament, the other half to ability. With Greig it's more like 90 per cent temperament. When the runs aren't coming, he still goes out and looks as though he is full of confidence. He bats the same way, throwing the bat at the ball and relying on power to rifle it through the cover field.

He is not afraid of the fastest bowling or the most intimidating bouncer. He accepts the challenge. I think he was a good captain who commanded the respect of his players. He was learning every day.

But he could never be rated a Test-class bowler. He was a trier, no more, but often broke stands and dismissed good batsmen who were set. His five wickets cost 67 runs apiece that summer and his successor as England captain, Mike Brearley, was probably right not to bowl him so much the following year against Greg Chappell's Australians.

Brearley had a difficult task following Greig as captain but was an instant success. He too commanded the respect of the players and was never apprehensive about asking anyone for advice. He is a thinking cricketer, sound in his tactical judgement and a better batsman than he is given credit for by some critics.

I was given a magnificent reception by the West Indian supporters as we left the field at the end of the 1976 series. Scores of them, many with flags and banners, escorted me off the pitch and I was most impressed. However, Bill Alley, my fellow umpire, seemed to be having a rougher time of it.

When we eventually struggled through the crowd in front to our room on the second floor of the pavilion Bill told me he had been buffeted. I was just about to say I'd been luckier when I put my hand in my back pocket and discovered that my money had gone!

I always take my money out on to the field, feeling that it is safer on my person. But I felt no resentment against the West Indian fans. In my view, they are the best cricket supporters in the world, knowledgeable, colourful and stimulating. Cricket is never dull with them in the audience.

I think they like me because they can identify with my name, 'Dickie' Bird. Occasionally when I look up I see them waving their arms like big birds and shouting 'Mr Dickie Bird'. I found a similar response when I attended multi-racial matches in South Africa.

11

One Summer

Professional cricket in England is like a travelling circus. There are about 250 performers, and we travel about 10,000 miles up and down the motorways every summer putting on a show at cricket grounds in cities, towns and sometimes even villages. Everyone knows everyone else and the spirit is tremendous. People say there aren't the characters that Sir Neville Cardus used to write about (or invent!) but I don't think that's true. The influx of the overseas players in 1968 not only brought in some of the world's greatest ever players but some fantastic characters.

One of them is Eddie Barlow, the South African who came to England to play for Derbyshire, and later captain them, in 1976. I knew Eddie from my days in South Africa. He has the same approach to cricket as the Yorkshireman: he's hard and abrasive and he's got to win. When I was in Johannesburg, the players used to get together at weekends for parties and most of us did a party piece. I did my big baboon act, 'Abba-Dabba' and everytime he sees me now 'Bunter' Barlow calls me 'Abba-Dabba'.

It was good business by Derby to recruit Eddie because he has raised them from bottom of the pile and made them a respected county. The players revere him and he is also very popular with supporters. Derbyshire have not had too much success with their overseas signings. They were unlucky with Lawrence Rowe and Srinivasaraghavan Venkataraghavan was not as big an asset as they expected. He caused havoc with the printing of the score cards! But Eddie was one of the best-ever overseas signings, well worth every penny of his salary.

One of the effects of the Packer intervention was that Bob Taylor, Derbyshire's reliable wicket keeper, finally made the England side after sixteen years of yeoman service to the game. Bob has been one of the best keepers in world cricket but Knott's consistency had kept him out until the tour of Pakistan and New Zealand. There is nothing to choose between them as keepers. Taylor is possibly better standing up and takes more stumpings. He is a quiet fellow, a good honest professional who gets on with the job. He deserves his promotion even if it has come near the end of his career.

I was looking forward to meeting Eddie at the start of the 1977 season because my first match on 4 May was Derbyshire v. Essex. Unfortunately, I was suffering from bronchitis and had to be replaced. I also missed the John Player Sunday League match between Northamptonshire and Derbyshire and I didn't start work until Wednesday, 11 May. The match was a Schweppes county championship game at Grace Road between Leicester and Worcester.

Though I had a mainly unhappy time there as a player, I never mind going back to Grace Road now because things have improved so much. Mike Turner, the secretary-manager, has turned Leicester into one of the major county clubs by his hard work and enthusiasm. The pavilion is almost unrecognizable and so is the square. One of his best moves was to sign Ray Illingworth from Yorkshire.

It was no secret in the game that Illy virtually ran the Yorkshire side for many years although he wasn't captain. He was the brains behind it. Ian Chappell once told me that he used to invite Illy out for a drink just to pick his brains. 'I did it deliberately to get him going,' he said. Illy is one of the game's outstanding thinkers and theorists. I know of no-one with his knowledge of the strengths and weaknesses of every opponent he meets. He is a master at field placings and also when to change the bowling. He's like a few other Yorkshiremen –

Clough, Bill Nicholson, Brian Sellers and many more – in that he doesn't throw bouquets around.

But do a good job and he will thank you. As in my day, Leicester have a number of Yorkshire players in their side. One of them is Jackie Birkenshaw, who was one of my best friends when we were at Headingley together. Jack was potentially the best youngster I ever saw but his temperament stopped him from fulfilling his potential to the full. He lacked confidence in his own ability. He was always darting off to the toilet before an innings and I was often beating him to it.

He's a jovial lad and on tours is the life and soul of the party. He has a stock reply when bowlers appeal for lbw and I am standing at that end. 'It's no use you bowlers appealing,' he will say. 'Dickie is my mate!' But there have been occasions when I have had to raise the finger. Two more Yorkshiremen in the side are Chris Balderstone, the batsman and slow left-arm bowler, and Peter Booth, the pace bowler. Baldy is a quiet person, and a fine all-round sportsman. He stands up straight and drives well on the offside. He is a fitness fanatic and still plays football professionally for Queen of the South.

Mike Turner is a good spotter of talent as well as a sound administrator and he made two more excellent signings when he brought Brian Davison and Paddy Clift to the club from South Africa. They can't understand back home in Rhodesia how Davison scores so many runs in England.

He rarely makes big scores in the Currie Cup whereas in England he is a punishing scorer. I think this is because cricket is played mainly at weekends in South Africa and he has to wait so long between innings. He is a player who likes batting every day. In some matches in South Africa, you have to wait two or three weeks before your next innings. The League cricket is of a very high standard and is in the form of two-day matches at weekends. All the top international players take part as amateurs.

When I first saw Paddy Clift as a schoolboy I thought he would go a long way in the game. He has a disarming approach to the crease. He doesn't look as though he is very quick but hits the pitch hard in the same way that Ken Higgs does and the batsman has to hurry his shot. He is the ideal type of stock bowler, the Max Walker type.

Also on their staff, Leicestershire have the left-handed David Gower, a future England batsman. He is another import. Mike Turner signed him from King's School, Canterbury. I have never seen anyone stand so still at the crease as this boy. It is a good sign. He has the gift of waiting for the ball to come to him and hitting it very hard indeed.

The Leicester *v.* Worcester match got started on the first day but heavy rain washed it out on the second and third days. It was a bad start to the summer. I spent most of my time laughing and joking with the Worcester players. Vanburn Holder had just been converted to a cover fielder and I told him he was another Clive Lloyd. Well, not quite. It is unheard of for a fast bowler to field in the covers but Vanny had a go and liked it. Most fast bowlers field third man or fine leg to give them a rest. You have to be very active in the covers and it is not the ideal way to rest between overs.

Some quick bowlers field close to the wicket though that is still rare. Chris Old and Mike Hendrick are two pace bowlers who are specialist close catchers. Both are brilliant fielders, among the best in the world. Their presence has strengthened England's catching capability enormously.

I left early for the next match, Somerset *v.* Nottinghamshire at Bath, beginning on 14 May. Bath is one of my favourite venues. The ground lies next to the river and pleasure park under the beautiful Grand Parade. The tents were up and Somerset had hired a temporary stand because the match following, in which I stood again, was against the Australian tourists. Fortunately, the weather was lovely: hot and hardly a cloud in the sky.

One of the first people I met was Brian Close, who was in his last season as Somerset captain. 'Closey' was the Churchillian bulldog of English cricket. Nothing frightened him and he stood up to the fastest of bowlers and let the ball hit him. But Brian was now physically past it and I think he knew it. In his

younger days, he would position himself close up at short leg
or point and take some incredible catches.

Against the Australians, he was still standing close in but
wasn't quick enough to react. Greg Chappell, who batted quite
magnificently, smacked him on the shin with one of his typical
on-drives and Close stood there as though someone had lobbed
a tennis ball against his leg. He didn't say anything, nor did he
rub the spot. But later when no-one was looking he pulled up
his trouser and his shin was up twice its normal size. It looked
like a rotten tomato. 'You want to go off with that and put
something on it,' I said. 'I'm all right, lad,' he replied. He
always calls me 'lad'.

I remember once when we were together in the Yorkshire
side at Worcester. We stayed in the Diglis Hotel, which is close
to the River Severn, and after a few drinks most of us were
ready for bed. But Close wanted to cash in on one of his bets.
He is a compulsive gambler. He will bet on two flies climbing up
a wall. 'Will anyone bet me I won't swim across to the other
side and back?' he asked.

I can't recall whether there were many takers but Close was
undeterred. It was pitch dark and he might well have been
diving into a log or the tide might have been out, but that
didn't worry him. He dived straight in, swam powerfully to the
other side and then back again.

He wasn't so lucky during the Australians' match at Bath.
The Mayor and Mayoress gave a reception for both teams in
the Roman Baths. It was a splendid occasion, with plenty to
eat and drink. 'Closey' was feeling pretty merry and decided
to dive into the deep end fully clothed. He went under and
showed no sign of coming up. Some of the other players got
anxious. They thought he might have hit his head and were
discussing how to rescue him.

The Australians thought it was hilarious. 'Let the bugger
drown,' some of them said. Suddenly, Close's bald head popped
up above the surface. 'Ha, ha,' he shouted. 'That fooled you.
Thought I was going to drown, didn't you?' Afterwards most
of the players changed into their trunks, including Close, and

had a swim. As he was stepping out on to a marble slab, Close fell awkwardly. There was a huge bang and we could all see he'd hurt himself. His knee puffed up and his shoulder was paining him. 'I'm out of match, lad,' he said to me. Next morning he went to hospital to be strapped up. He could hardly walk.

Back at the ground, he insisted on changing into his cricket clothes in case he was needed. Somerset's youngsters, particularly Brian Rose the new captain, batted so well that he didn't have to go in but when he declared the innings closed in the late afternoon, he insisted on going out at the head of his team. This time he fielded a yard or two farther away from the bat, at gully.

Close did a wonderful job in his years at Somerset. He turned a struggling county into one of the best young sides in the county championship and he did it virtually without any bowling. As he told me after he had announced his retirement, he had no spin bowler after Brian Langford retired and no fast bowlers. To win championships, you need bowlers of class and Somerset had none. Yet they still managed to bowl sides out by making do with what they had. The batting was good enough. Close said he had the best batting side in the championship and, with Viv Richards to spearhead it, he was probably right. In 1976 Close was criticized by some people close to the club for driving his players too hard but that was the Yorkshire way and he was proved right.

One of the Somerset youngsters, Ian Botham, matured so quickly that he won a place in the England side. Botham has an aggressive approach to cricket. Some detractors have said he is over-confident, even arrogant, but cricketers need confidence to reach the top. I have seen enough fail for lack of it. Botham will, I think, become a better batsman than a bowler in time.

Somerset definitely had the best batsman in the world in their 1977 side: Viv Richards from Antigua. Whatever length you bowl to him, no matter how perfect it is, he will murder you. His one weakness was said to be his impulsiveness and he admits that Close did much to help him cure this fault. Viv says

I am his favourite umpire because he always makes a big score when I am there at his matches.

But I have seen him fall to slow left-arm bowlers who flight the ball. Once he was dismissed twice in a match against Nottinghamshire by the Indian spinner Doshi, who is one of the few bowlers in the championship who uses flight. Johnny Wardle once said to me that he got all the great players out in his time by flighting the ball and varying his pace. It made them hit too early and get caught.

Most slow bowlers these days bowl flat. There are few left who are masters of flight. Bishen Bedi was in a class of his own but now that Northampton have dispensed with his services we shall not be seeing him again except when he is touring with India. Derek Underwood bowled without much flight against Richards in the 1976 season but I feel Viv is vulnerable against the slow left-arm bowler who varies it because he goes for his shots. Now that he has curbed his impetuosity, this remains his only weakness.

He is a lovely lad, very friendly and always smiling. He has my taste in caps and is frequently asking to borrow my white one. They are a bunch of nice lads at Somerset. One of my favourite cricketers is Graham 'Budgie' Burgess, the ex-Millfield School boy who had his testimonial in 1977. 'Budgie' is one of cricket's most honest and true professionals. If he gets a nick he won't stand there, he will help you by walking straight away. Derek Taylor, the wicket keeper, is in a similar mould. He is a fine keeper, not far behind Bob Taylor, whom I rate the best with Alan Knott.

Somerset beat the Australians in a high-scoring match on a superb pitch but Greg Chappell wasn't worried. It was the first game his side had managed to finish because of the bad weather which they had experienced up to then and some of his batsmen had valuable practice. Greg himself could have had a hundred before lunch. He was 99 not out and he pushed the remaining balls back. He is not a record chaser. David Hookes also got a big score with some huge hits but I thought his footwork might let him down against better bowling in

Tests, and so it proved. It was an entertaining match played in ideal conditions.

It was notable for the fact that I called Jeff Thomson sixteen times in six overs for over-stepping. He was having a lot of trouble at the time. A lot of people came up to me afterwards and asked what Thommo said. Was he upset? Did he swear? Well, Jeff Thomson is one of the quietest, best-behaved fast bowlers I have ever come across. Never once did he object. All he said was, 'How's it now?' He marks a line about eighteen inches behind the bowling crease and measures his run from that. But when he drops his marker at the end of his run, he goes off wide for a few yards. I told him I thought that was the trouble and I think I may have helped him because as the Test series got under way he bowled far fewer no-balls.

I remained in Bath that night because I was standing in the Lancashire *v.* Somerset Benson and Hedges match the next day. With so many competitions and playing conditions, the umpire has to be on the alert to make sure he has the appropriate regulations. The Lancashire match brought my first meeting with Colin Croft, the six-feet-six-inch fast bowler who'd done so well for the West Indies against Pakistan.

He came up to me all smiles. 'How delighted I am to meet you,' he said. 'You are *the* Mr Dickie Bird, aren't you?' I thought he was pulling my leg. The Lancashire players might have put him up to it. But he was genuine. 'I have heard so much about you at home,' he said. 'They all talk about the great Dickie Bird. I thought you were an old man, not a young man.'

I wished I could be so complimentary about his bowling but he sprayed the ball all over the place and David Lloyd had to take him off. He wasn't quick although the Yorkshire batsmen told me that later in the year he was very quick against them. Despite his erratic bowling, Lancashire succeeded in winning against Somerset. There was a funny moment when he bowled a short delivery at Peter Denning and it struck the batsman in the stomach. Croft shouted, 'How was that one, Mr Dickie Bird?' The players doubled up with laughter.

I had the next six days off and went home to relax. There are periods when the umpire has time off and I always do the same thing: sit at home with my feet up. The following Saturday I had the Worcester *v.* Australians three-day game at New Road, Worcester, one of my favourite grounds. I always stay at the Shakespeare pub in the town centre and walk across the bridge over the River Severn to the ground. Basil D'Oliveira invariably greets me the same way when I arrive at the pavilion.

'Here we are again, Dickie,' he will say. 'We should be lying out on a beach somewhere with a gin and tonic. But here we are, worrying about whether it's nicked the glove, whether the keeper caught it cleanly. It's not right, is it?'

Vanburn Holder, the West Indian pace bowler, is another of Worcester's characters. He is a very popular man. The telephone is always ringing for him. In one match I no-balled him and he came back up the pitch, stabbed his foot on to the crease and crouching, looked up and said, 'I'm all right here.' I replied, 'Yes, you are but the trouble is back here. You've gone over the return crease on the back foot.' He took it like a gentleman.

Jim Cumbes, the pace bowler who used to be a goalkeeper with Aston Villa, once caused a riotously funny moment in one of my matches when he bowled to Sarfraz and as Sarfraz lobbed an easy catch back, he failed to get a hand to the ball. I said, 'I thought you were supposed to be a goalkeeper.' The fielders roared with laughter. 'He's just as bad in practice,' said one. Club cricketers aren't the only players to drop easy catches! The Australians duly beat Worcester. Greg Chappell was again in superlative form. The runs simply flowed from him.

I was back on familiar mining territory in the next match, Derbyshire *v.* Gloucester in a county game at Ilkeston. Keith Stevenson, the twenty-six-year-old Derbyshire pace bowler, hit me under the chin in his back swing as he was bowling and I buckled to my knees. This sometimes happens to umpires. What with looking for the bowler's feet, the ball and the batsman, it is impossible to watch out for the bowler's arm!

I soon recovered and next ball Stevenson appealed for an lbw against Julian Shackleton, son of Derek Shackleton, the ex-Hampshire and England bowler. I was fit enough to say 'That's out.' Gloucester developed into one of the country's leading sides under the captaincy of Mike Procter. I have known Procky since his days at Hilton School in Natal. He is a world-class cricketer and a fine competitor. I once asked Geoff Boycott which bowler gave him most trouble and he said, 'Mike Procter. He bowls such a good line and length and he nips it back on you.'

Procky was at his quickest in the South Africa v. Australia series in 1970–1 and though he has slowed down since, he remains an exceptional fast bowler. He had a serious knee operation and most of his friends thought he would never bowl fast again. He bowled off spin for a time, and not badly either, once taking 8–16 for Rhodesia v. Transvaal. But in 1977 he was back off his full run and whipping batsmen out again. He destroyed Hampshire in the Gillette Cup on a good batting wicket at Southampton, a game I saw on TV. He was urged on by cries of 'Kill, kill, kill' as he raced in to bowl. Being the cricketer he is, Procky helps create atmosphere.

I stood in the memorable Lancashire v. Gloucester Gillette Cup semi-final at Old Trafford which ended at 8.50 p.m. in the half light and I remember that I had to warn him for slowing the game down. The crowd were chanting and he was waving his arms about as though he were conducting an orchestra.

'Keep it rolling, Procky,' I said. 'It's not me,' he said. 'It's the crowd.' I had to be firm. 'Yes, but it's you that's keeping them at it.' Lancashire won through that amazing over of hitting from David Hughes. I still don't know how he saw the ball.

Sadiq Mohammed, the opener from Pakistan, is a chirpy, witty little man. In the match at Ilkeston, he was caught by the New Zealander John Wright off the bowling of Fred Swarbrook and though it was bat and pad, it was obvious he was out. He stayed at the crease and I had to give him out. After the close of play he sought me out. Umpires usually have a drink with the players afterwards. We are not like soccer referees who are not encouraged to socialize. 'I'm sorry I didn't walk,' said Sadiq. 'I was going to.'

'What do you mean?' I said. 'You were standing there for five minutes. It was slow death.' Zaheer Abbas, Gloucester's other Pakistan Test player, is a nice quiet man who smiles a lot and clearly enjoys what he is doing. He must be the best slow wicket player in the world. The West Country pitches suit him. He seems to wait for the ball and then leans back and punches it through the offside. David Shepherd, 'Shep', is a salt of the earth player in the 'Budgie' Burgess class. I have never known him not walk when he knows he is out.

He was put in an embarrassing position in that Ilkeston match. Stevenson was bowling and as the ball passed down the legside I thought to myself, 'That ball has gloved him.' It went through to wicket keeper Bob Taylor but Taylor didn't appeal and nor did Stevenson. I was at square leg.

At the end of the over he said to me, 'Did you see that fourth ball, Dickie, it brushed my glove? I couldn't walk because no-one appealed.'

That weekend the one-day internationals, England *v.* Australia, started. I was down to umpire in the third and last one at the Oval with Ken Palmer, the former Somerset bowler. There was a big crowd and towards the end, with Australia chasing the runs, it started to rain. The rain fell so heavily that we should have come off. We asked both captains, Mike Brearley and Greg Chappell, who was batting at the time, and both said they were willing to keep going in an effort to finish the match. Despite the conditions, the worst I ever encountered (my boots were full of water), Chappell carried on in magnificent fashion and ended with 125 not out.

The next day was the Queen's Silver Jubilee Day and the TV cameras would have to be shifted from the Oval! Pools of water formed on the pitch but somehow we managed to finish. The significant point about that game was that neither side's bowlers bowled a short ball all day. The real ammunition was being saved for the Tests.

My next job of work was the Benson and Hedges quarterfinal between Kent and Sussex at Canterbury, one of my first-choice grounds. The pitch for that 55-over match was about the best I'd seen all season

Kent won before a full house through the efforts of Christopher Cowdrey, son of Colin, whose 114 was a brilliant innings in true one-day style. Christopher is like his father in manner and personality, a real gentleman, but his batting differs considerably from his father's. He's more of a legside player. His sportsmanship was shown when he caught Kepler Wessels, the Sussex opener from South Africa, on the boundary and though it looked good he signalled 'Not out'.

With so much money to be won in limited-overs cricket, there is a great temptation not to help the umpire. I have found few occasions myself where players have deliberately tried to take advantage of a situation. Chris Cowdrey's gesture may be looked on as unprofessional (it certainly would be in football) but to me it was an encouraging example of how the sporting traditions of cricket are still preserved in this country despite the increased commercialization of the game. At the close, I went up to him to congratulate him.

Afterwards, I undertook the 250-mile, lonely drive back home ready for Yorkshire v. Nottinghamshire at Headingley on the Saturday, but I needn't have rushed. The first two days were washed out. Neither captain was prepared to risk his faster bowlers. I met Geoff Cope, Yorkshire's England off-spinner, and we had a laugh about the time he tried to slip me a double gin when he brought the drinks out in a match against Sussex at Headingley. I thought there was something wrong when he handed me what appeared to be an orange. I took a sip and spat it out and the players laughed. I am not a shorts man.

Cope is a nice, friendly lad and I am pleased that he managed to break through to the England side after the troubles over his action. He has been filmed several times but after going to Johnny Wardle to have one or two little points straightened out, I consider his action is now no different from that of any other off-break bowler. In my view, no slow bowler who tweaks it can be expected to have a ramrod straight arm. It's simply not physically possible.

Sunday, 12 June, was Nottingham *v.* Yorkshire at Trent Bridge, a match made more interesting by the sight of Geoff Boycott bowling in a cap. I said to the Yorkshire lads, 'It's Emmott Robinson reborn!' Emmott always bowled in a cap. Not many bowlers do nowadays. Boycott laughed along with the others. He is not the worst bowler in the country by a long way. He has dismissed some very good players, Graeme Pollock among them. In fact, he can reel off most of the names of his victims and his bowling figures if he is asked. He is wary about his back, otherwise he would bowl more.

I rate Boycott highly as a captain. He has done an immeasurable amount of good for Yorkshire cricket and particularly its younger players. They freely admit they owe him a huge debt. He is always helping and advising. If he had been Yorkshire captain earlier in his career, in the days when they won the title in 1959, 1960, 1962, 1963, 1966, 1967 and 1968, he would have been one of the most successful captains of all time. Since 1968, when overseas players were allowed into the county championship, he has laboured under the handicap of competing against sides with world-class players in their ranks. Take Procter, Sadiq and Zaheer out of the Gloucester side, Barry Richards, Gordon Greenidge and Andy Roberts out of Hampshire, and Mushtaq and Sarfraz out of Northampton, and see how these counties would have fared against Yorkshire. Yorkshire have refused to sign overseas players because they think it is contrary to the best interests of Yorkshire and England cricket and that is their right. But it probably cost them medals.

After the Jubilee Test match at Lord's, I had a few days off before going to Chelmsford for the Essex *v.* Sussex county championship match which started on Saturday, 25 June. There was still no sign of a repeat of the blazing summer of 1976 when the Chelmsford outfield looked the colour of a sandy beach! Essex have a beautiful new pavilion and I like going to Chelmsford. The players are such a great set of lads, some of the biggest jokers in cricket.

Tony Greig, the Sussex captain, wasn't laughing when he threw me the ball during the Essex first innings and complained that it was out of shape. Changing the ball had become the most boring ritual in English cricket. It was going on all the time, and not always because the ball was genuinely out of shape. It is impossible to make the perfect ball and there are some bad ones about. But some captains were using it as an excuse to change a ball which wasn't helping their bowlers. If the bowlers were running through a side, no captain would ask for the ball to be changed. But if they were being hammered, inevitably the captain would try to change it.

The authorities at Lord's were wise to this and advised umpires not to change the ball unless absolutely necessary. I looked at the ball Greig gave me – a top quality, quartered ball, shiny one side, rough the other – and threw it back. But Greig kept on about it.

He asked for another inspection. The other umpire was Tom Brooks, the Australian who with Sang Hue, the West Indian, were the overseas umpires on the first-class list at the time. Tom is an amiable, friendly man and a conciliatory person but he agreed with me that there was nothing wrong with the ball.

'Right,' said Greig. 'I am going to complain about this. I'm serious. You will live or die by the decision you make.' I replied, 'Well, in that case, it looks as though I am going to die because I am not going to change it. Let's get on with the game.' We never heard any more about it and Essex went on to score more than 300 runs off that particular ball.

On the last day, Keith Pont, the Essex 12th man, brought out a champagne bottle and champagne glasses for drinks. Ken McEwan, the South African batsman who kept scoring hundreds in June, had won a magnum of champagne from a national newspaper and wanted us all to share his bounty. Ray East was, I remember, the person who cracked the bottle. It would have made a great picture for the Press but the photographers who were there didn't notice what was happening until it was too late.

Ray East, the thirty-year-old left-arm spinner from Manningtree, is the leading play actor in English cricket. He was doing stunts and cartwheels long before Derek Randall brought some gaiety and fun into Test cricket. Some people say that if he didn't fool about so much he would be a better cricketer. Well, his 8–30 against Nottingham at Ilford on 26 May was the best bowling performance of the 1977 season. He is not that bad a bowler.

Ray East is the only bowler in England who actually gets down on his knees and prays when he appeals to me. He will plead, 'Please, Dickie, how was that?' I don't know if he does this with other umpires but he has always done it with me because he knows I will respond to a joke.

The Essex players are always talking. No matter where a player is fielding, he will shout out to a colleague things like 'Who's coming on now then? Who? Not him!' David Acfield, the off-spinner, is one of the noisiest. The captain, Keith Fletcher, is one of the quietest. Keith knows the game and is an intelligent talker about it. McEwan, whom I saw play as a schoolboy in South Africa, is one of the most improved cricketers in the world. England could do with a middle-order batsman of his calibre.

Sussex had John Snow in their side in that match but he made no impact. I didn't think he was trying. If he respects an umpire, he will give him no problems. I can't remember him worrying me. But if he doesn't respect you, well, he can give you a hard time. Whenever I have no-balled him he usually says, 'You've got bloody good eyesight, Dickie.' True, I don't wear glasses and I pass my eyesight test every year!

12

One Summer Ends

By the end of June, I was back at the big Test grounds. Filled to capacity during Test matches, they are stimulating places to be but with a few hundred people on a dull day in midweek, they can be soul-destroying. It is generally agreed on the circuit that the Oval is one of the most depressing of the large grounds.

John Edrich was supposed to be in his last season as Surrey captain but I never believed him. For the past seven years, whenever we met in the middle he would say, 'That's it, Dickie, this is my last game. I'm giving up.' But he would be there again next time. There have been few braver men in English cricket than 'Edie'. He has sustained many serious injuries – nearly all his fingers have been broken at one time or another – but he keeps battling away.

Though the Oval is hardly uplifting, we had a laugh in the Surrey v. Warwickshire match after the then Warwickshire captain, David Brown, chairman of the Cricketers' Association and one of the game's stoutest characters, set Surrey a very reasonable target on the last day after dictating events for the previous two days.

Surrey looked as though they were going to get the runs and Bob Willis started bowling bouncers at Geoff Arnold, the Surrey fast-medium bowler and former Test colleague. Although there is nothing in the laws as such, bowling bouncers at tailenders was said by the International Cricket Conference to be in the wrong spirit of the game. The faster and shorter Willis bowled, the harder Arnold hooked him for four. I ought really to have intervened. There were far too many short deliveries. But Arnold was in no difficulty, he was relishing it.

Eventually Arnold shouted down the pitch, 'What about this short-pitched bowling?' I think he meant it as a joke. 'The way you are hitting him out of the ground, I'd say you're not too bothered, are you?' I said. When he came up to my end in the next over, Arnold whispered, 'I'm glad you didn't step in. It's my finest shot!'

Surrey proceeded to win the match and afterwards, Edrich, their captain at the time, said, 'I couldn't understand it. All Willis had to do was pitch it up and bowl straight.' Robin Jackman was playing in that match and his presence made me recall an incident earlier in my career when he bowled a bouncer to Gordon Greenidge of Hampshire and Gordon hooked him high over square leg. Instinctively, I started running towards the boundary to make the catch. It dropped over the rope for six and shamedfacedly, I raised my arms to signal from my new position not far from the boundary!

From the Oval, I went to another ground where midweek attendances are not as high as they used to be, Edgbaston, the most modern and most spacious of the major grounds. The match was Warwickshire v. Essex and Warwickshire evidently needed to improve their bowling rate. Sides that fail to exceed 19·5 overs an hour are fined and to avoid paying out £500 themselves, the players often use dull games to step up the rate. This was one of them. Warwickshire bowled their 100 overs just after lunch, some two hours odd ahead of normal time. They did it by the expediency of bowling off ridiculously short runs. Willis, for example, bowled off two yards. The Essex batsmen scored boundary after boundary. It was farcical.

There are some very sociable people in the Warwickshire side. David Brown I rate as one of the nicest cricketers ever to don flannels. He had a big benefit, nearly £30,000, and deserved every penny. Eddie Hemmings is the joker, always chattering away. I was sorry that John Jameson retired. He was a punishing batsman and one of the best cricketers in the

E

business at telling the umpire how many no-balls he had
missed when he was non-striker.

While the Second Test was being played at Old Trafford, I
was at Worcester for a county match against Glamorgan. Each
incoming batsman would tell me the score. Twelve months
before, Collis King and I met after the 12th man incident in the
Trent Bridge Test and ever since then he calls me 'Birdie'. He is
a jolly cricketer who failed to play as well for Glamorgan as he
did for the West Indies. That may be because he was used to
faster pitches. Glamorgan's tend to be slow turners.

Collis succeeded another Barbadian at Glamorgan, the fast
bowler Gregory Armstrong. Greg was really fast, but lacked
control. I had many experiences with him, often giving him the
final warning for running down the pitch. He was a frequent
over-stepper as well.

While having a drink with some of the Australian cricketers,
I asked them which batsman in county cricket impressed them
most (this was before Geoff Boycott made his comeback). They
all replied, 'Alan Jones of Glamorgan.' In his long career, Alan
has only once represented England, in a Rest of the World
match in 1970.

The Test was still on when I went down to Worcester again
for a Schweppes county match, Worcester *v.* Northants. Bishen
Bedi was playing and he always asks me to stand back, after an
incident when he stood on my foot. He marks a spot and says,
'Can you stand there?' It is up to the umpire where he stands.
He is only being polite when he agrees to move to suit a bowler.
But Bedi is such a nice man I wouldn't dream of upsetting him.

Northants have one of cricket's more priceless characters in
the Pakistan pace bowler Sarfraz Nawaz. He is so good, cutting
it off the seam and swinging it away, that I am surprised that
Kerry Packer didn't sign him. In one match, Sarfraz kept
switching from over to round the wicket and back again. In the
end I was so confused that I signalled a wide. 'What wide?' he
said. I forgot that he had gone back round the wicket!

When we come out at the start of play, he always asks me
which end I am taking. 'You good umpire,' he says. 'I go to

other end. No lbws from you. Captain! The other end please.'
He calls me 'Dickie Dido'. Sarfraz has had many jousts with
fellow fast bowlers. In a Northampton game against Somerset
Allan Jones, who was then with Somerset, got upset and began
bouncing the ball at Sarfraz. Sarfraz didn't mind because he
is a proficient hooker, but he shouted, 'Your turn will come.
When you bat, I will knock your head off.' George Pope, the
other umpire, and I had to intervene but I distinctly remember
Allan Jones backing down on that one.

Sarfraz had a similar experience with Jeff Thomson in 1975,
I was told. Thomson was angered by two short balls in succession from Sarfraz and intimated that he would be letting Sarfraz
have one in return. 'All right,' said Sarfraz. 'Take your pads off
and give them to me and you can try it now. Give me your bat.'
As he walked back to his mark, he said, 'I rang the curator at the
local cemetery this morning. He said there is one grave left. It
is for you.'

The umpires once had a discussion at Lord's about Mushtaq's
reverse sweep shot. Sometimes he will change from right hand
to left hand as the ball is being delivered and sweep the ball
through the slips. It is not covered in the laws so no action was
taken. John Dye, the left-arm pace bowler Northants signed
from Kent and released at the end of the 1977 season, has the
same conversation with me whenever I stand in one of his
matches. 'Good morning, Dickie,' he says. I reply, 'Keep back
that front foot, Doctor. And two, don't run down the wicket.
And three, be a good boy.' He says, 'Okay, Dickie, let's go.'

I asked some of the Northants players once why he is called
'Doctor'. Apparently he was given the name by the Kent
players because he was always in the treatment room. He knew
so much about it that they christened him 'Doctor'.

David Steele doesn't say a lot but when he is batting sometimes repeats the phrase, 'Fight on, you must fight on to the
death.' That sums up his approach to batting. Jim Yardley,
the wicketkeeper–batsman who joined Northampton from
Worcester, has the reputation of being one of the game's leading squirters. Whenever I see him play, he manages to squirt the

ball through the slips and not get caught. In one match, Lance
Gibbs of Warwickshire was so annoyed that he put three gullies
in position and said, 'Now get it through there!' Next ball,
Yardley played forward, edged, and the ball streaked along the
ground through the gully fielders. Gibbs threw the ball down.
'I can't bowl to this man,' he said. 'It's impossible.' That may
have hastened Gibbs' decision to retire and go home to Guyana!

I had a few days' rest before the Benson and Hedges final at
Lord's on 16 July. I stayed at my usual hotel, Dormers in Talbot
Square, which is a meter zone. You always have to be up early
to put your ten pence in the meter, but early rising is never a
problem for me. The competing teams were Kent and Gloucester and I thought it would be an evenly balanced game. The
toss is always very important if it is a good wicket. Procter won
it for Gloucester and decided to bat. Kent's bowlers, particularly Bernard Julien and the youngster Kevin Jarvis, were very
wayward and the Gloucester openers Sadiq and Andy Stovold
lashed into them. The game was won before lunch. Once Bob
Woolmer got himself caught on the boundary, needlessly having
a swing, Kent fell further and further behind.

The contest itself gave fellow umpire Lloyd Budd and me
no trouble, but the Gloucester fans did. There were continual
soccer-style chants, and as Procter bowled he was accompanied
by the now familiar 'kill, kill, kill'. I do not think this is a good
thing for cricket. The West Indians supporters were the first to
bring noise to English grounds and in the main' it was good-
hearted expression of enjoyment. But some of the shouts from
the Gloucester contingent, or a section of their fans, were un-
pleasant and unwholesome. Too many people had too much
to drink. Afterwards, there were beer cans everywhere. The
authorities in football have had to ban the sale of drink at some
grounds and I think it could happen in cricket if this unsavoury
trend continues. It is more often than not found in one-day
matches where the spectators know there is going to be a result
in the day.

Some policemen had their helmets knocked off at Lord's and,
worse still, some policewomen had their skirts ripped off. At tea

Jim Fairbrother, the Lord's groundsman, asked me to be sure to bring the stumps in at the end. I was at square leg when the winning run was struck and I could see what was going to happen. I turned and ran as fast as I could for the pavilion, leaving the stumps and bails to the hundreds of onrushing Gloucester supporters to fight over.

Mike Procter invited me into the Gloucester dressing-room for champagne. I had a couple of glasses before setting off for the 180-mile drive home. Halfway up the M1 the big end went in my car and I had to be towed off the motorway. The car needed a new engine and I had to borrow another vehicle.

I had a week to argue it out with the garage (I had only just bought the car) before the next assignment, Lancashire v. Nottinghamshire at Liverpool. The Liverpool ground is unattractive but the pitch is of good standard and Lancashire often get good crowds there. On Saturday the attendance was 14,000, a better gate than the county would get at Old Trafford.

There was an amusing incident when Jack Simmons was bowling. The ball struck the batsman on the hip and he turned and said very quietly, 'How was he, Dickie?' Entering into the spirit of it, because the appeal was obviously frivolous, I shouted, 'Not out.' David Lloyd, then captain, asked me what was wrong. I said, 'He's appealed for that.' The players all laughed. Cricket is never dull when Jack Simmons is playing. He came into the professional game rather late, at the age of twenty-seven, after being a League cricketer and he enjoys every minute of it.

Lloyd was a good captain and a fine player of spin bowling. He is a very likeable man. Frank Hayes, his successor, thinks a lot about the game and is very personable. I was sorry that Farokh Engineer retired. He was one of my favourite performers, a real extrovert.

After the Third Test at Trent Bridge, I went to Edgbaston for the Warwickshire v. Yorkshire match which started on Saturday, 6 August. There were runs to be made on that Edgbaston pitch. Boycott scored a hundred and so did Jim Love. Twenty-two-year-old Love is another good young Yorkshire

batsman. He is a powerful driver off the front foot and a quick
scorer and he also got a hundred.

The batsman who scored the fastest runs, however, was Chris
Old. He reached his century in thirty-seven minutes and it was
the fastest century of the season by far. I think he was rather
embarrassed by it all. He kept saying to me, 'It's not my fault,
is it? You've got to hit that kind of bowling.'

Not only were Warwickshire trying to bowl some quick overs,
they were also looking for a declaration from Yorkshire. White-
house, who doesn't bowl much, bowled twelve overs and
Kanhai, another non-bowler, sent down three. Eddie Hemmings, the regular off-spinner, bowled fifteen. Spectators may
have thought it was splendid entertainment but there was an
element of farce about it. Though half the first day was lost
through rain, a total of 819 runs was scored for the loss of
fourteen wickets. Boycott declared – but there was no chance
of a result.

That Sunday I did the short hop across to Nottingham for
the Nottingham v. Warwick John Player match and after the
Yorkshire game was over, flew to Australia to make a Volkswagen advertisement on TV. That meant I missed Northamptonshire v. Middlesex at Wellingborough. On my return, the
weather put us all out of work again. I was scheduled for the
Gillette Cup semi-final between Middlesex and Somerset at
Lord's but it was washed out on the Wednesday. A fresh start
was planned for the Thursday but it was still raining. On the
Friday it was just as bad and Mike Brearley and Brian Close
and the two club chairmen met with Donald Carr, secretary of
the Test and County Cricket Board, to discuss a new time and
place.

It was mutually agreed that we would play on Wednesday,
24 August, the day before Brearley was due to lead England
in the Final Test at the Oval. That meant the Middlesex v.
Somerset county match down to start at Lord's on that day
would have to be played on another date. It was – at Chelmsford, and Kent were upset because their match on that date
was affected by rain. I left Lord's early for Canterbury for the

Kent *v.* Somerset match. There was no hope of playing after
the first day. The players practised at the indoor school and
Norman Graham regaled us with stories about how well his
benefit was going. He is a popular cricketer and his popularity
was being reflected in the takings. Les Ames said he had never
seen the ground so wet in his fifty years with Kent.

Rain stops play is the most boring part of an umpire's life.
The players play cards, or watch racing on TV or just talk. But
the umpire usually stays in his room with his fellow umpire
talking and reading. I don't read books myself and I am not a
card player. I prefer talking. That summer there was much to
talk about: the Kerry Packer affair being the chief subject. The
players had mixed views and it was no surprise that the voting
was so close at the Cricketers' Association meeting at the end
of the season. There were those who said the Packer men were
right to try and make as much money as they could from the
game, and others, like Ray Illingworth, who saw it as a threat
to the established game.

Back at Lord's on 24 August for round two in the Middlesex
v. Somerset Gillette Cup semi-final, it was the story as before: no
play because of rain. Most of the day the players sat in the
dressing-rooms discussing ways of settling the tie. The semi-final
is the big one. No-one feels it worse than a player on the losing
side in a semi-final. Now we faced the prospect of having to toss
a coin. Most players were in favour of some test of skill. One or
two wanted something laid on in the indoor school. Others
suggested going out to the middle in football boots and playing
at all costs. Brian Close was firm. 'We're not going to play in
farcical conditions,' he said. He had more at stake than anyone.
It was his last season and his last chance of winning a medal in a
one-day final.

On the Thursday it was still raining. Still no chance of a start.
Officials started checking with other grounds to see if the game
could be switched. They rang Hove, Canterbury and Derby.
Hove and Canterbury were too wet, so Derby seemed the best
choice. We arranged to meet early on Friday morning and
drove off to our respective hotels. The sun was out when I woke

next day, but when I arrived at Lord's the square was still wet, and in normal conditions the game would have been off again.

The captains both wanted to play, and so did the Test and County Cricket Board officials. Someone had rung the London Weather Bureau and the forecast was a bright morning followed by heavy rain from the west at around two o'clock. Weather forecasts are not always reliable but this one appeared to be pretty firm about the time the rain was expected to hit London.

Mike Smith, the Middlesex vice-captain who was standing in for Brearley, agreed with Close that it would have to be a shortened game. Close wanted ten overs a side, and it was easy to see his view. He had Viv Richards, perhaps the world's best batsman, in his side and if Viv came off, Middlesex wouldn't be able to catch Somerset. Mike Smith wasn't going to agree to that. He wanted thirty overs a side, or roughly four hours' cricket which would have taken us past the 2 p.m. deadline. Finally it was agreed to play fifteen overs. It was hardly a satisfactory way of settling one of the season's most important matches, but there was no alternative.

The ground staff covered the square in sawdust and off we went, Somerset batting first. Richards was lbw 8 to a full toss from his West Indian Test colleague Wayne Daniel. Daniel let himself go and bowled really fast. Somerset's batsmen got themselves out for 59 and Middlesex were left with an easy target which Clive Radley and Mike Gatting achieved by sensible cricket. Close was thoroughly downhearted as he left Lord's.

As the players were driving off, a heavy shower fell at 1.55 p.m., which was five minutes before the predicted time. But the skies cleared afterwards and play would have been possible again. The Weather Centre spokesman told a newspaper reporter, 'We never said it would rain continuously. All we said was that there would be heavy showers in different parts of London and there were.' You can't rely on weather forecasts! Play was possible nearly all day in the Oval Test on the south side of the River Thames, less than four miles away.

I saw Phil Edmonds, the England slow left-arm bowler, as I was leaving. He asked me where I was going to and I said

Bournemouth, for Hampshire *v.* Kent. Kent could still win the championship, so could Middlesex or Gloucester. I asked him what he thought was the best way. He said the M3, or was it the A3? I saw a sign to the A3 and took that. I ended up in Portsmouth, not really the best route. I arrived an hour or two behind schedule.

It wasn't, I was sure, a plot by Phil Edmonds! In any case, the match was rain affected. Kent were in a sticky position when we called it off. Hampshire might have been in contention for the title themselves but for injuries. Their gentleman of a captain, Richard Gilliat, one of the best captains in the country, was out for some time with a fractured cheekbone, and Barry Richards and Andy Roberts both missed matches. In the end, the championship finish went right up to the last hour of the last day and Kent and Middlesex shared the title, the first counties to do so since Surrey and Lancashire ended level in 1950. It had been a sparkling start for Schweppes. As for me, it was the end of another enjoyable summer. But if only it hadn't rained so much!

13
Packer

On the Friday of the Jubilee Test I was sitting alone in the umpires' room at Lord's when there was a knock at the door. A man was standing there, a household name in cricket. 'Can I have a word with you?' he asked. I asked him to come in.

He asked me if I was interested in umpiring the Kerry Packer Supertests in Australia later in the year. I said I had never given it a thought. He went on to say there would be a lot of money involved, so much that I would need an account in Switzerland to put it into bonds. I was stunned. Naturally I have a bank account but I am not very well off, nor have I ever wanted to be. I am happy with my life in cricket. I own my bungalow and my income is sufficient to cover my expenses. I have never looked on happiness as being associated with wealth. To me happiness is being in a game you love and meeting and talking with fellow cricketers. It may be a small world, but it does for me. It has given me a chance to travel to many places and meet some interesting people.

The man asked me not to divulge his name and I am keeping that promise, even now that it is all over. I was too taken aback to say too much. 'I can't say anything at the moment,' I said. 'That's all right,' he said. 'Don't make your mind up now. You have plenty of time to decide. We'll contact you again.'

'Will these Packer Tests come off?' I said. 'Yes,' he said. 'They will be a very great success.' We discussed how much money I would make. He quoted some figures in Australian dollars. 'What's that in pounds?' I asked. 'About £10,000 a year,' he replied. It wasn't a firm figure but I would receive one-third as a down payment. The deal took in coaching as well as umpiring.

Kerry Packer was arriving in London at the time to attend talks with the cricketing authorities at Lord's. He was booked in at the Dorchester, not far from Lord's in Park Lane. I had never met him. His plans to set up pirate matches were the talk of cricket. Everywhere I went on the circuit, the players were discussing Packer and his implications for the first-class game.

The man shook hands and left me to think. Lloyd Budd was the other umpire in the Jubilee Test and I didn't tell him anything about it. I had been asked to be discreet. I went home after the Test finished on the Tuesday, tossing it around in my mind as I drove up the motorway. I knew there could only be one answer. I was flattered to receive such an offer but I was too content with my life in England to risk giving it all up for money.

The next night the telephone rang. It was one of Packer's men. I hadn't given him my number. He said I would be needed to start on 24 November and would have to stay in Australia until March. 'Don't rush it,' he said. 'I'll call you in two weeks.'

The meeting between Packer and the International Cricket Conference delegates took place at Lord's the following day. Packer arrived at the Grace gates in an Austin Princess. Richie Benaud, one of his consultants, was sitting in the jump seat. On TV, Packer was very dogmatic after the meeting broke up without agreement. 'After this, I will take no steps to help anyone,' he said. 'It is every man for himself and devil take the hindmost.'

He was reported in the newspapers as having said that he conceded several points but when he asked for one back, the ICC wouldn't bend. He was quoted, 'The concessions I made today were considerable. I got to the stage of suggesting a working party to discuss details, but the stumbling block was that the Australian Board convinced the other countries that we should not be given the privilege of TV rights in Australia.

'I said I would go back under control of the Board, shorten

our tour and withdraw from the scene completely. I came prepared to compromise. Compromise means two people coming together and giving. I was giving.' Asked what would happen if the authorities banned the players he had signed, which was being talked about, he said, 'If that happens and our players are victimized, our attitude will harden. We will extend our operations.'

This convinced me, if I still had any doubts, that I would be outlawed from Test cricket if I accepted the Packer offer. I would never stand in a Test match again. Packer had declared war.

Jack Bailey, the secretary of the International Cricket Conference, issued a statement. It read,

The sub-committee of representatives of Test match playing countries met today with Mr Packer and his associates, Messrs Taylor, McNichol and Benaud. The sub-committee advised Mr Packer they would be prepared to recommend to their respective Boards that the Boards approve his privately promoted professional series subject to the following conditions:

1. The programme and venues are acceptable to the home authority and the length of programme to be six weeks, unless otherwise agreed. The matches would be under the control of the home authority and played in accordance with the laws of cricket.

2. No player to participate in these games without the prior permission of his home authority. This permission would not be withheld unreasonably.

3. No teams taking part in these matches could be represented as National teams, i.e. not Australia but possibly an Australian XI.

4. Players contracted to Mr Packer to be available for Test matches, first-class fixtures and other home authority-sponsored matches where there was no clash.

5. The home authority must be able to honour all contractual commitments to existing sponsors and advertisers.

It was put to Mr Packer that if he could agree to negotiate within the broad framework of these basic points, a sub-committee would be appointed to endeavour to reach agreement on a mutually agreeable programme of matches.

Mr Packer was adamant, however, that he was not prepared to consider entering into any negotiations unless he was given an absolute guarantee now that his company would be granted exclusive television rights to cover Australian cricket at the conclusion of the Australian Board's current contract in 1978–9.

Representatives of all countries present were unanimous that no member country should be asked to submit to such a demand either now or in the future. The Australian representatives indicated they were prepared to recommend to their Board that they give consideration to the principle of exclusive television rights, not previously granted in Australia, and if approved Mr Packer's company would be given an equal opportunity with others to submit an offer. This proposal unfortunately proved unacceptable.

That morning I went to see my solicitor and personal friend, Duncan Mutch, the same solicitor used by Geoff Boycott, in his Barnsley office. Duncan is a cricket fanatic and a member of Lancashire (both Geoff and I have overlooked that because he is a good solicitor). I told him I didn't want to harm my career, and he said I ought to ring Donald Carr at Lord's.

Duncan put in the call and Mr Carr's secretary said he was in a meeting. It must have been the meeting of delegates which preceded the afternoon session with Packer. Not an ideal time for me to call! Duncan said it was very important and could Mr Carr call back when he came out of the meeting.

At 2 p.m., Mr Carr returned the call and Duncan told him about my Packer offer. He didn't seem surprised, nor did he try to influence my decision. He asked to be kept informed. For the next two weeks the Packer business played on my mind and I lost weight, though it didn't affect my umpiring.

The next call from the Packer men came on 13 July, a

fortnight before the ICC meeting at Lord's which decided to ban all the players who had signed for Packer, now numbering more than fifty, including the whole of the West Indies side (though Alvin Kallicharran was later to withdraw) and most of the Australian Test squad. I told the caller that I had given his offer a great amount of thought but had decided to turn it down. He said, 'It's your decision and yours alone. Thanks very much.'

Someone who had helped me with advice was a cricket philanthropist, William Harrison, who had been a lawyer until his retirement. Mr Harrison, now ninety-two and still able to go to matches, advised me against signing.

I rang Donald Carr and told him the news. 'Well done,' he said. He sounded enthusiastic and pleased. That Saturday I was due at Lord's for the final of the Benson and Hedges Cup and I arranged to see him and Publicity Officer Peter Lush to talk about how the news was to be released.

Lloyd Budd was again my fellow umpire. He could see that I was more fidgety than usual but I didn't tell him until the tea interval. There were several Packer players on the field, Alan Knott, Asif Iqbal and Derek Underwood from Kent and Mike Procter and Zaheer Abbas from Gloucester. We never talked about Packer or the future of cricket. It was too tense a game of cricket.

In Mr Carr's office later, I worked out a Press statement. 'I have informed the Test and County Cricket Board,' it said, 'that I have received and turned down an offer to umpire in the proposed series of international matches to be played in Australia this winter. In coming to my decision I stress strongly my loyalty to English cricket which I have been part of for many years and I don't wish to take any action which would be prejudicial to my position as an umpire in Test and County Cricket.'

We had a gin and tonic and I left for the celebrations in the Gloucester dressing-room. The statement was issued on the Monday morning and made most of the evening and morning newspapers in the next twenty-four hours.

For the rest of the week, letters poured into my house, all congratulating me on rejecting Packer and staying loyal to established cricket. One was from an old lady from Sheffield and

I reproduce it because it touched me deeply. Money can't buy feelings like that. The letter went:

> Dear Mr Bird, This is from an old lady of nearly eighty-nine years of age but I want to tell you how you bucked me up when I heard you on the telly last night and read about you in the *Star*. Congratulations and good luck to you where-ever you are. I must tell you how refreshing it was to meet what I call a real Englishman. They are few and far between these days.
>
> That Tony Greig wants to get back to South Africa where he belongs. As you will guess I am a true cricket fan. I used to visit Bramall Lane when they played cricket there and have seen most of the greats of the game. I just love it and even at my advanced years I never miss cricket on the telly.
>
> Thank you for being so loyal to England and to the game. Good luck to you. Yours sincerely, Mrs H. Forbes. PS This is the first fan letter I have ever written.

The day after the ICC meeting to ban the players, I was at Trent Bridge for a Test. The Australian players made jocular remarks. 'You must be loaded to turn that offer down,' one of them said.

At tea-time on the Monday, I was having a cup of tea and a scone in the umpires' room when an attendant came with a message to ring a number in Sydney, Australia, on reverse charges. I said, 'It must be someone taking the mick.' The attendant said it was genuine. 'Doesn't the fellow in Sydney know I'm in the middle of a Test match?' I said.

I sought out Rodney Marsh at the end of the day's play and asked him what was the best time to make the call. He said nine o'clock in the evening. That night I spent the evening with Norman Mee, a friend of mine, who runs the Trent Bridge Inn next to the ground. I often have a steak at the TBI at Test match time. Norman took me to his office and we made the call from there. The number rang out a long time before a voice said, 'Hello, who is it, you've just got me out of bed.'

I asked what time it was out there and he replied, 'Six in the morning.' Rod Marsh had slipped up somewhat! I apologized for getting him up but he forgot all that when I told him I was Dickie Bird. The man's name was Bill Currie, managing director of Berry Currie Advertising. His company wanted me to do an advertisement on TV for Volkswagen cars. Could I come out immediately? Well, not immediately, I said. England still had to get 189 to win the Test. He said what about before the next Test, could I squeeze it in? They were willing to pay me around £1,000, or almost half as much as I made from a whole summer of umpiring. It was a sizeable sum, but after the taxman had finished I was left with only £550!

I said I was keen to come, but would have to fix it with Lord's. I did have a free week before Headingley. 'That's great,' said Bill Currie. 'And don't forget that white cap. They go barmy here over that white cap!'

Bill told *The Age* newspaper, 'I nearly fell out of bed when he said he wanted to do it. I told him we were looking for someone associated with cricket and all the players seemed over-exposed. We started looking for personalities who weren't players and there weren't really any here. We looked at the English and then thought "why not an umpire?" Dickie gets on well with the Aussie players. He's got a tie presented by the 1975 team which he says he wouldn't sell for £3,000. This bloke lives and breathes cricket. He's almost a father figure to fellows like Marsh and Lillee.'

Donald Carr soon cleared me to go, providing I was back in time for the Gillette Cup semi-final, my next scheduled match. I had a tourist ticket when I flew out on 8 August but the captain of the Qantas Jumbo jet recognized me and I was given a seat in the first-class section. I was given VIP treatment, me, just an ordinary umpire! The Headingley Test was due to start that week and the newspapers thought I was flying to Australia because I had changed my mind about joining Packer. Bill Currie's representative in London told me to say 'no comment' to the newsmen at the airport because they didn't want the rival channels to know. It increased the speculation that Packer was involved.

After an exhausting flight, I was driven by chauffeur-driven car to a hotel for a wash and brush up, then straight on to the TV studio. I did the commercial that day, dressing up in my regulation gear and reading out the script about VW cars. It was put on TV that same night – on Channel 9, which is Kerry Packer's station! I had some connection with Packer after all. The evening newspapers had pictures of me with the story. 'Umpire's secret out', said one headline.

The next day there was a message for me: could I go to the studios to see Dennis Lillee? Lillee was commentating on the live film from Headingley, for which Channel 9 paid the Test and County Cricket Board £150,000 for the exclusive rights in Australia. Dennis has always been one of my favourite cricketers. I was dog tired, but I went. It was exciting watching Boycott from Down Under, sitting next to the bowler who could have made so much difference to the series.

I asked Dennis if he missed it. 'Deep down, I do, Dickie,' he said. But he thought Packer's matches would be a success. All the Packer men were loyal. Also commentating from the studio was the former Australian opener Keith Stackpole and I exchanged a few stories with him. He is a very amusing companion.

He told me about the time he was given out caught behind in South Africa in a Test when he hadn't touched the ball. It was the last ball before lunch. He missed it and took his gloves off to make for the pavilion when there was an appeal. The umpire, perhaps thinking Stacky was giving himself up, promptly put his finger up. 'I've never walked in my life,' he said.

There was also that classic Stackpole story from a Test in the West Indies when he gave Uton Dowe, the Jamaican fast bowler, some fearful stick at Sabina Park. Dowe was fast, but very erratic. He kept dropping short and Stacky, one of the game's outstanding hookers, kept smashing him into the crowd. Rohan Kanhai, the West Indian captain, took Dowe off after six overs in which he had conceded 63 runs, a colossal number for a Test bowler in his opening spell.

Later in the day, when Stackpole was still at the crease,

Kanhai decided to give Dowe another try. As Dowe was marking out his run, a voice in the crowd shouted, 'Kanhai, haven't
you heard the 11th commandment? Dowe shalt not bowl.'

Though I had only a short time in Sydney, it was a memorable visit. Bill Currie gave me a huge koala bear to take home as
a souvenir, and on the plane I sat next to a woman who said, 'I
recognize you. I am so glad that you turned Packer down. All
cricket lovers in Australia feel the same way. Please take this as
an appreciation.'

She handed me an Australian version of the Queen's Silver
Jubilee coin. I still have it. The koala bear is still at home. I
call him 'George' and he occupies a chair of his own. We were
delayed at Bombay on the way back but I arrived at Heathrow
in good time for the Gillette Cup. In fact, it was postponed anyway because of the weather. I need not have worried.

My view about Packer hasn't changed. I don't think circus
cricket will ever replace the real version. I think Test cricket is
the greatest kind of sport there is. It has everything, drama,
tension, the build up, the let down, the needle and peak of
physical achievement. The only event that compares with it is
the Olympic Games and the Olympics only come round every
four years.

I cannot see that Supertests can succeed when they are
played under different laws from the ones that have been used
so successfully in just over a hundred years of Test cricket.
Once you start tinkering with the laws, the sport declines. The
Americans have found this out with Team Tennis. The prizes
have gone up whereas the players' enjoyment from playing has
disappeared.

Packer has legalized bouncers to tailenders. I can never see
that that is right. He also installed microphones so the comments of the players could be heard. Players were encouraged
to comment on the umpire's decisions – until they convinced
Packer it was a bad idea. To my mind, that was a prostitution
of cricket.

One innovation in the one-day game that does have some
merit, however, is the drawing of two circles with a thirty-yard

radius from each wicket with each side having nine fielders within the circle. This is an idea copied from South Africa. It makes captains maintain a more attacking field in the opening ten overs. Too often in one-day cricket the captain falls back on a defensive field with no-one near the bat. The idea is to contain, not so much to get batsmen out. I can never understand why this tactic was adopted in England. I think Ted Dexter may have pioneered it in the early days of the Gillette Cup. Sussex were successful in the early sixties in the competition and other sides have followed their example.

The best way to slow down the run rate is to dismiss batsmen and your chances of getting them out are improved if you have more, not fewer, fielders in catching distance.

Previous instances of series with Rest of the World sides have shown that the public aren't so interested in these artificial matches. The real battle, country against country, is the one that commands most interest. I can understand the thinking of the cricketers who have signed for Packer. First-class cricket is only half a working life. When the player retires he still has twenty years or so to work and often he isn't trained for anything else except cricket. Most cricketers, even those who have had large benefits, suffer from this feeling of insecurity.

The decision to say No to Packer worried me not because I had any doubts about turning it down but because so much money was involved. I never had a benefit in my cricketing career. Nor did I make any perks from endorsements.

Though I do not have a family like many of the players who received offers, my mortgage is probably as large as theirs, £69 a month, and my rates are probably bigger, £268 a year for my small bungalow. And on top of that I pay much more in tax as a single man. I had nothing to gain by turning Packer down except esteem from those people in cricket who are against what Packer has done to the game.

Bob Willis has had his income more than doubled by rejecting Packer's offer. Boycott has signed a £50,000 contract with Slazenger's. I do not begrudge them their money but I would just like it to be recorded that it was a considerable sacrifice for me to remain loyal to English cricket. Even now, with the High Court rescinding the TCCB and ICC ban and making the Packer players available to continue playing county and Test cricket, I have no regrets. You do what you feel is right for yourself. I am happy to remain in English cricket.

14

Boycott's Test

The night before a Test match, I rarely sleep properly. I am too tense. England *v.* Australia at Trent Bridge, 1977, was my fourteenth Test but I felt the tension just as much as before my first one. I think some nervous excitement is a good thing. Your performance is better if the adrenalin is flowing. Most of the players are affected by it too though some are in such a state that they can't do their talent justice. I haven't reached that stage yet!

I rise early on the morning of a Test, usually at 7.30, and I say my prayers. I do not go to church much but I believe in God. At 9 a.m. I go to the ground to inspect the pitch. The hotel at Nottingham is just across the road. The pitch at Trent Bridge looked a very good one with pace in it. Geoff Boycott was making his comeback and I thought to myself that if he made a start, the Australians would have difficulty in getting him out on it. He'd be feeling the tension too. I saw him at practice about an hour after I arrived. He winked at me and I said, 'Good luck.' I don't know if an umpire is supposed to say something like that!

If I had to ask a batsman to bat for my life, Boycott would be the man, ahead of all the other great players. In the middle, he rides tension superbly, giving little sign that he is nervous. But he is nervous. All great players are because cricket is the great destroyer. A good player can receive the unplayable delivery first ball just as frequently as a bad player.

I think Boycott worries about things privately though he never lets on. Criticism affects him and I think he was upset by the attempt to unseat him as Yorkshire captain at the end of the 1977 season. He also has a dread of being injured or getting ill.

I don't know how he reduces tension at the start of an innings but I remember well how I did it in my first Test, which was at Headingley in 1974. Ron Griffith, the West Indian from London who is a popular figure at the Test grounds, kept up a stream of advice. 'Don't let those players bother you, Mr Bird,' he said, and such like. Without thinking I pretended to take my jacket off and hand it over to him. He started to come on the field, the crowd erupted – and it broke the tension.

The weather was perfect at the start of the Trent Bridge Test, not a cloud in the sky. I inspected the boundaries. The regulations say the ropes shouldn't be more than ninety yards from the pitch and not less than fifty yards. In the middle the ground staff were putting the stumps in. Some groundsmen pour water into the holes before they insert the stumps so that when the stumps are hit, they fly out of the ground and it's more spectacular.

At 9.45 I began to change ready for the 11.30 start. I never leave anything until the last minute. The umpires' room at Trent Bridge is one of the smallest rooms in the building, no bigger than a box bedroom, and hardly big enough for two chairs and a table. It is situated next to the stairs and the noise of people running up and down the stairs can be distracting if you like sitting quietly to think, as I do when I have finished changing.

We have a small weighing machine to weigh the balls. Just after ten, the umpires go to the captains to choose the balls. There are a number of different makes. This time Greg Chappell and Mike Brearley both chose a Duke's Grade A, made in England and hand-stitched. They cost about £15 apiece. We also have a number of spare balls which have been used for a set number of overs so that if a change is necessary, we can provide a ball with a similar amount of wear.

When the captains went out to toss at eleven o'clock, David

Constant and I were in our room. Umpires don't preside at this
ceremony. The 12th man comes in to say which team has won
the toss. Chappell won and decided to bat, the obvious decision
in the conditions. At 11.15 the first bell goes. Time for one last
visit to the toilet. 11.25 the second bell. Time to go.

As we walked through the pavilion doors and down the steps
out on to the ground, we were greeted with loud applause. I
think that was because I had just rejected the offer to join Kerry
Packer. The public were acknowledging my loyalty to the
English game and I was affected by it. There were tears in my
eyes. I took deep breaths in and out, my way of dealing with
nerves. My sleeves were rolled up as usual.

I asked Connie which end he wanted. 'I'll have the camera
end,' he said. The BBC cameras were at the pavilion end. Ends
never worry me. You have to change in the next innings anyway. Bob Willis opened from my end. 'Now then, Dickie,' he
said. 'How are you?' Bob Willis always says that. It is a ritual
with him. The England bowlers didn't bowl well and the
Australian openers Rick McCosker and Ian Davis put on 78
for the first wicket.

McCosker scored 2 and 0 at Old Trafford but kept his place.
The Australians don't drop good players lightly. He played
well. So did Davis before he was out to an atrocious shot. Davis
was livid with himself for giving a simple catch to Ian Botham
at mid on off Underwood. Botham's first spell in Test cricket
was unimpressive. It had been a good morning for Australia.

The umpires have lunch in the players' room at Trent
Bridge. Both teams eat in the same room, though at different
tables. There are rarely any exchanges between the rival
players during meal times. A hot meal is provided at Nottingham, and a good one too. The organization by the Nottinghamshire club was first class throughout and it was one of the best-
run Test matches in my experience. But the best lunch in the
cricket circuit is served at Lord's. None of the other grounds
can match it. They even give you a choice.

Many players don't eat too much at lunch time. Boycott
never does if he is batting. Nor do the bowlers. Fred Trueman

always had a pint and nothing to eat. I don't know what Ian Botham had that first day but when the match resumed he started taking wickets in an amazing fashion and his 5–74 bowled Australia out for 243. Greg Chappell was the big one. Botham bowled him when he dragged a widish delivery on. The ball wasn't really swinging much.

Mike Hendrick made as fine a catch as I have seen to dismiss David Hookes in the gully, diving full stretch to his left and holding the ball in both hands. It is uncommon to see that kind of catch held in two hands. Kerry O'Keeffe's 48 not out was the only correct batting after McCosker and Davis. The others had played some ghastly shots.

The Royal Standard had been hoisted and was fluttering in the breeze, which meant Her Majesty the Queen and His Royal Highness Prince Philip had arrived at Trent Bridge to meet the teams. The 12th man came out to tell us that the Queen would be coming out at the end of the over. We lined up and were presented in turn. The Queen asked me if I was feeling tired after another long hot day in the middle. I said I wasn't. 'Are you enjoying it?' she asked. 'Yes, m'am, very much,' I said. She has a relaxed way about her which puts you at ease.

As she came to the end of the England line, Mike Brearley called out, 'Three cheers for Her Majesty, hip hip . . .' The Queen cut him short. 'Just a minute, Michael,' she said. 'Philip isn't here.' Philip was still down the line, talking to one of the players!

England safely saw out the remaining minutes and were 7–0 at the close. Boycott, looking keyed up, was struck on the pads but the ball was going down the legside and the appeal was turned down. I had a shower in the Australian dressing-room – there are no separate showers for umpires at most grounds – and went off to be entertained to dinner by some insurance friends of Connie at Nottingham's most expensive hotel. I left at ten and went straight to bed. I still tossed and turned, though it had not been a particularly taxing day for me.

Friday was another sunny day with a packed crowd. Boycott came out with Brearley to a noisy reception. The crowd was certainly on his side. Brearley fell to a Hookes catch off Len Pascoe and Woolmer, shuffling back and across as he does, was lbw to Pascoe. The ball struck him below the knee.

'How's that one, Dickie?' cried Pascoe. 'That's out, Lenny,' I said. Pascoe is a nice lad and a good competitor. He was very upset with the allegations by former England captain Ted Dexter in the *Sunday Mirror* that he threw.

In my view, there was never any suggestion that his action was illegal. I thought he was a fine bowler who could have taken more wickets on the tour if he had pitched the ball up another yard or so. I think he concentrated too much on banging the ball in and trying to get lift.

At one stage during the day's play, Pascoe got rather worked up and bowled a succession of short-pitched deliveries. Boycott, the main recipient, ducked out of the way. Finally I had to intervene and tell Pascoe to cut down on the bouncers. He took it well. 'Fair enough, Dickie boy,' he said.

Pascoe tries so hard that he often mutters under his breath. There was one occasion when I heard him saying, 'I'll knock shit out of them.' I said, 'Now then, Lennie, you'll not knock shit out of anyone.'

Max Walker was equally frustrated when he bowled at Boycott. After several overs of finding the middle of Boycott's bat, he said to me, 'What do I bowl to him next, Dickie?' 'Bowl him a hand grenade,' I said 'That will blast him out.'

Derek Randall was next man in and his local crowd gave him a deafening reception. He is very popular, not just in Nottingham but everywhere he goes. World-wide fame after his 174 in the Centenary Test in Melbourne earlier in the year hadn't changed him. He remains a very nice, shy, unassuming lad, a natural fidget and a clown on the field. I could see he was a mass of nerves as he came to the crease.

He was trying to be matey. 'Hello, Marshy,' he said to Rod Marsh. Marsh was less than friendly. 'This isn't a tea party, you know,' he said grimly. Randall asked for two legs as his guard. Most English players take leg or two legs whereas the bulk of the Australians prefer centre.

He had barely got started before Boycott ran him out. I was
at the bowler's end and as soon as Boycott played the ball back
just wide of the playing pitch to Jeff Thomson's right I could see
there was no run in it. But Boycott had shouted 'run' and was
on his way. He was never going to get back if Randall said No.
At first Randall hesitated. Then he set off.

Thomson, who is an agile fielder, especially to his own bowling, turned and bent to retrieve the ball. It wasn't hit very hard
by Boycott. If Thomson had missed it, I doubt whether it
would have gone twenty yards. It was extraordinary that Boycott should want to run. The pressure on him must have been
so intense that he'd acted quite out of character. The Australians were shouting to Randall, 'Stand your ground.' They
wanted Boycott to be the one who was run out!

Boycott was almost past Randall before Randall set off.
Derek is a fast runner but he had no chance of beating Thomson's accurate throw to Marsh standing behind the stumps.
Marsh knocked all three stumps out of the ground in his exulta-
tion and Randall was out. Boycott was at my end, his appearance shell-shocked, his face drained. He threw his bat down,
then his gloves and held his head in his hands. 'It was my fault,'
he said. 'I've run him out in front of his own supporters.'

There were some boos among the cheers and sympathetic
applause for Randall as he walked in. Some cricket lovers
hadn't forgiven Boycott for withdrawing himself from the
England side. This incident must have turned more people
against him. You could imagine what his critics were saying:
it was another example of his selfishness. In fact, as he explained at a press conference later, he hadn't run many batsmen out in the previous three years. He had set out to cure this
self-acknowledged fault in his game and in that time he'd been
run out by others more times than he'd run colleagues out.

Tony Greig was the next batsman in and he came up to Boycott to console him and urge him to keep going. Some sections
of the crowd were giving Boycott some stick but he survived
and at lunch was 13 not out after two and a half hours at the
wicket. It was an incredible piece of concentration. He didn't

go up to the players' room for lunch. He sat in the dressing-room
instead.

Then came the moment which I considered the turning point
in the series. When he was 20, Boycott got an outside edge to a
delivery from Jeff Thomson and the ball went straight in, and
out of, Rick McCosker's hands at third slip. Thomson was again
at my end. He bowled that one from wide of the crease, which
he does often, and Boycott had no need to play it. But he was
getting impatient. Greg Chappell, standing next to McCosker,
went down on his knees in frustration. 'Oh no,' he said. By Test
match standards it was a very catchable catch.

At the end of the over Chappell walked past and I said, 'That
could cost you the series,' and he replied, 'You're right.' He
looked most unhappy. If Boycott had gone then, England
would have been out for a much lower score and the Australians
would probably have won the match. Catching was the
difference between the sides as Mike Brearley said at the end of
the series. I couldn't remember seeing England's close catchers
holding so many good catches, or Australia's dropping so many.
Also England's outfielding was superior to Australia's.

When he was next at my end, Boycott said, 'I shouldn't have
played at that. I've got to do something now.' I've never seen a
cricketer looking more determined. England could have been
87-6. Greig went, his leg stump knocked out by Thomson. The
Australians, like the West Indians, got their fast bowlers to
bowl yorkers on the line of middle and leg to exploit Greig's
habit of lifting his bat before the bowler bowls and tying himself
up in knots. I could never understand why he continued to do
it. He was yorked time and time again.

Alan Knott joined Boycott and played what must have been
his greatest innings for England. He played shots from the start
and the crowd rose to him. They were starting to love Boycott
too and by the close these two had changed the whole course of
the match. Knott's 135 was the best I'd seen him play. Boycott's 107 was his thirteenth Test hundred. He'd willed himself
to it. It was a test of his temperament as much as his ability and
he'd come through. When Knott reached his hundred, and

the crowd were on their feet to him, I said, 'When you go with Kerry Packer, you'll miss all this.' There were tears in his eyes. 'You could be right,' he answered.

Although Trent Bridge is a good batting wicket, no English batsman had scored a century there since Denis Compton's 184 in 1948. Knott eventually fell to Thomson, a peculiar-looking shot to a wide delivery which landed the ball in the hands of Ian Davis at third man. 'I've strangled him!' said Thomson. And he added, 'If he'd let that one go, it would have been a wide.'

Boycott's long innings ended with a similar delivery from Thomson. He played a lazy shot and this time Rick McCosker held the chance. Ian Botham arrived to start his first Test innings and edged nervously to Greg Chappell – but Chappell, one of the world's finest slip fielders, dropped it. England were all out 364, a lead of 121.

McCosker played the Boycott role in the Australian second innings, holding an end up by sensible defence and hitting out at the loose balls. He used a Gunn and Moore bat, made locally in Nottingham. All the Australian players use English bats, either Gunn and Moore or Gray Nicholls. They get fitted out when they arrive at the beginning of a tour. At the end of Saturday's play, the Australians were 112–2, still needing 9 to make England bat again. Chappell, their leading batsman, was victim of a delivery from Mike Hendrick which he dragged on. He did that more than once in the series.

I spent the day relaxing on Sunday. Most of the players also take it easy though a few, chiefly the Australians, play golf. On Monday morning I was at the ground early to see the groundsman, Ron Allsopp, cut the pitch. The umpires have to ensure that the cut is always the same, not too much grass taken off and not too much left on. The pitch is cut on alternate days in Test matches.

McCosker and David Hookes put on 94 for the 3rd wicket when play resumed and Mike Brearley was beginning to look anxious. Brearley is never afraid to consult his players. He is constantly seeking other views but leaves no-one in doubt that his is the opinion that counts. He has a pleasant, easy approach

to the job and is not overbearing or dictatorial in any way.
Tony Greig was a ferocious chewer of gum and the Australians
chew gum as well. But Brearley doesn't. Brearley was criticized
for not putting Geoff Miller on earlier but I thought he was
right. The pitch suited pace, not spin. Brearley's captaincy was
impressive.

At 42, Hookes was lbw and I gave him out. Hookes never
walks straight off. He always looks at the umpire first even if
it is a thick edge. He gives the impression of wanting a last-
minute reprieve.

When he first arrived in England, he came with a big reputation. Some experts said he was another Neil Harvey. The way
he struck Greig for a succession of fours in the Centenary Test
earned him a name as a stroke player of considerable promise.
But Hookes never fulfilled that promise in England, basically
because his footwork was wrong.

Batting is all about footwork. It is essential to get the foot in
line with the ball. But Hookes rarely moved his feet far enough.
He hit the ball from where he stood. On good pitches, when the
ball came straight on, it was possible to get away with this. He
did so at Bath. But against bowlers of Test quality it is vital to
get in line and leave no gaps. During the series Greg Chappell
and the senior Australian players were continually giving him
advice on this point. He is so young and inexperienced that if
he irons out this technical fault, he could still become another
Neil Harvey.

Walters was soon back in the pavilion with Hookes. He
smashed a short ball from Greig straight at Randall at cover
and Randall – another young batsman whose footwork needs
improving – made a convincing case of trying to show it was
harder than it looked. Meanwhile, McCosker reached his 100
in the classic manner, flat hooking a delivery from Willis,
pitched outside the off stump, over square leg for six. A
stupendous shot!

Richie Robinson sprayed a few shots around in unorthodox
manner before Underwood had him lbw. McCosker went for
107 and Marsh, playing in his fiftieth Test, was superlatively

caught at slip by Tony Greig diving to his right as Brearley dived the other way behind him. Marsh got 0, the same score as in the first innings, so he had made a pair. I felt sorry for him. One of his finger bones was chipped and his hands were covered in bruises stopping the 90 m.p.h. deliveries of Jeff Thomson.

Kerry O'Keeffe was left on 21 not out, to follow his 48 not out in the first innings, when Australia were finally all out for 309, setting England 189 to win. O'Keeffe was dropped for the next Test, unluckily in my view. He had batted soundly in both innings and though his bowling was expensive, 0–99, he had the excuse of having a bruised spinning finger. He could well have been tried as an opener.

Brearley handled Willis superbly, bringing him back at crucial times to take wickets. Willis took 5–88 and was England's spearhead. I thought he was much more mature than he used to be, more willing to respond to the call than in previous years. Later it was revealed that he had been experimenting with hypnotherapy to improve his performance. While in Australia in March for the Centenary Test, he met Dr Arthur Jackson, a member of the Australian Sports Medicine Federation and an expert in the comparatively unknown art of using hypnotherapy in sport. Dr Jackson gave him two twenty-minute recordings which Willis played back on a portable cassette recorder to hypnotize himself. He used the tapes during the Trent Bridge Test and was reported to have said, 'It is impossible to say how many of my wickets I took as a result of this but there is no doubt that the session with Arthur Jackson has made me a better bowler as well as a more relaxed and confident person.'

Willis said he was worried by not being able to sleep during the previous winter's tour of India. 'Before he put me under, I was feeling the tensions and stresses of the tour,' he was reported. 'When I came out of my hypnotic state, I felt relaxed and quiet. The buzzing had gone from my head and I stopped worrying.

'But there is a lot more to the treatment than just learning to relax. If I hadn't been to see Arthur Jackson, I would not be as fit as I am now. He advised me to run five miles a day. He also improved my concentration and gave me confidence. I used to dread having a ragged old ball thrown at me during the last session of a day in a Test match and being asked to get a wicket. Now I relish that sort of situation.'

Dealing with tension is a subject I have thought of a lot myself but I have never used any aids like hypnosis or sleeping pills. I think it is something you have to conquer yourself. I have always believed that but if Bob finds his solution from a recording, well, that is his business. He is to be admired for making himself into a much more reliable bowler. He finished the Australian series the leading wicket taker with twenty-seven wickets at an average of 19·77. Unlike some fast bowlers, Bob is a very equable person. He rarely swears or curses. He's the gentle giant among fast bowlers.

Boycott batted before the close on Monday which gave him some kind of record of having batted on all five days of the Test when he resumed on Tuesday morning. He was on the field for all but 1¾ hours of the Test. For a man of his age, thirty-seven, he is amazingly fit but, except for prolonged net practice, he doesn't do a lot of training. Next day, he and Brearley batted relentlessly against an Australian attack that became increasingly discouraged. Brearley didn't suffer in comparison to Boycott.

Jeff Thomson, Pascoe and Walker bowled magnificently. Boycott plodded on. It was no time to be taking risks. The 100 stand came and went. It seemed only a matter of time. During lunch Alec Bedser, chairman of the selectors, asked Nottingham officials to check the weather forecast because apparently rain was expected. They came back to say that the forecast was not too good for later in the afternoon. Brearley was told, and he decided to force the pace after lunch. He tried to slog Walker and was bowled for 85. The 1st wicket stand put on 154. Alan Knott was promoted to number 3, got two overthrows and was then well caught by O'Keeffe in the gully off Walker. Greig went next, trying to hit Walker out of sight.

Three wickets had fallen in a mad rush, but there wasn't a cloud in the sky. Boycott refrained from joining in the scramble, calmly picking up runs when he could. Derek Randall came in to play some fine shots, there was no run out, and together they saw England past the target. Boycott was 80 not out. He didn't look tired either.

Marsh took his gloves off and shook hands with Connie and me, a nice gesture I thought. I had the stumps in my arms and gave them to Greg Chappell. The players always take the stumps for souvenirs. Boycott said, 'Here, where's ours?' 'I don't know where they are,' I said. 'I think Connie's got yours.' I think he got a stump in the end. He deserved one.

Back in the dressing-room, I took my shoes and socks off and put my feet up before joining the England players for a glass of champagne.

15
One-day Finals

When one-day cricket was first introduced into the English professional cricket calendar in 1963, the editor of *Wisden* wrote, 'There is no doubt that provided the competition is conducted wisely it will attract great support in the future and will benefit the game enormously.'

Wisden called it 'The Knock Out Competition' although it was, as it is now, sponsored by Gillette. Well, it has been conducted wisely and few alterations have been made in its format since that time. It was so successful that another Cup competition was brought in, the Benson and Hedges Cup, and both have continued to thrive. Some Kerry Packer supporters claim cricket administration is out of date but few sports have made such radical and progressive changes in England as cricket in recent years.

The John Player League, with its sponsorship and larger attendances, was launched in 1969 and the Benson and Hedges Cup in 1972. Overseas players were admitted to the county championship in 1968, reviving interest around the counties, and in 1977 the championship was at last sponsored.

Gates at Test matches were falling for much of the time in the sixties but in the seventies this trend has been dramatically reversed. In 1977 the house-full signs went up four days in a row at Nottingham, unprecedented since the days of Bradman.

As a player, I took part in the first Gillette Cup tie ever staged in this country. It was a preliminary round match between

Lancashire and Leicester at Old Trafford on 1 and 2 May 1963. These sides had been bracketed together at the bottom of the championship table the previous season. Rain delayed the start and when play at last began, Maurice Hallam put Lancashire in but it didn't work out.

Lancashire scored 304–9 off their sixty overs with Peter Marner scoring 121 to qualify for the first ever Man of the Match award. Marner was a powerful hitter, unlucky not to play for England. His temperament was against him. He was rather impetuous sometimes, getting himself out by hitting across the line. Leicester made 203 in reply. H. D. Bird b. Statham 7. Hallam 106.

Brian Statham, 'George' to his colleagues, had all of us in trouble except Maurice Hallam. His twelve overs cost 28 runs and he captured five wickets. There were few better one-day bowlers than 'George'. He was like Mike Holding of the West Indies – fast, though not as fast as Holding, and very straight.

If you edged him through the slips for four he would accept any apology graciously. 'Don't worry,' he used to say. 'That's four more runs for you.' His England partner Fred Trueman said something rather different!

My first Gillette Final as an umpire was Lancashire v. Middlesex in 1975, the thirteenth final. The crowd that day was 24,195, with seemingly just as many of them supporting Lancashire as Middlesex, the home county. Umpires have an extra responsibility in one-day matches: they have to record the number of overs bowled by each bowler on a printed card issued by the Cricket Office at Lord's. I cannot remember anyone making a mistake and allowing a bowler an extra over. There are enough checks. The scorers would soon tell you.

The captains are always asking how many overs bowlers have remaining, even though it is up on the scoreboard. Most of them want to save their opening bowlers' final overs for the end of the innings when batsmen are aiming to score at their fastest. It is harder to slog a good bowler than an average bowler. A couple of hours of keeping it tight can be thrown away in the final overs unless the captain has planned properly.

It was a slow pitch for that 1975 final and David Lloyd, the then Lancashire captain, asked Middlesex to bat because some dampness still remained from a heavy shower which fell earlier in the week. It is a source of amazement to me that the Lord's groundsman Jim Fairbrother and his staff manage to prepare so many good pitches from the overworked Lord's square.

By the time the Gillette Final is played, inevitably in the first week in September, there is often little grass left at the ends but there are never any complaints about the pitches from the captains. The groundsmen, like the scorers, are the unsung characters of cricket, men who are never in the public eye unless they make a mistake. Few cricket lovers praise a good pitch the way they applaud the performance of a cricketer. No-one says to the scorer, 'Well scored.'

The county scorers are all professionals, often ex-players, and they travel around with the teams. Cricket *aficionados*, who can recite *Wisden* from page 1 to page 1122, wouldn't be able to name the seventeen scorers of the county clubs. I doubt if anyone could.

Lancashire's pace bowlers, Peter 'Plank' Lever, Peter 'Leapy' Lee and Bob Ratcliffe, all moved the ball about in the opening overs and Mike Brearley and Mike Smith were both pinned down. No-one has been able to tell me how Lever got his nickname. 'Plank' usually signifies being wooden, or thick, but Lever was one of the brightest people in professional cricket. 'Leapy' Lee's nickname is more obvious: it derives from his action.

Smith, Brearley, Radley and Featherstone all went by the time the total reached 64 and if Larry Gomes, the West Indian Test player who was later released to allow Wayne Daniel to play in county matches, had been caught at 2 Middlesex might have been out for a record low score in a final. But the chance was missed and Gomes went on to make 44, top score in the Middlesex total of 180–8.

Fielding and running between the wickets are so important in one-day matches. Often matches are won and lost by fielding, like the World Cup Final played at Lord's that same

summer. Another vital consideration is field placings. The
captain has to know his opposition and where they play their
shots. Ray Illingworth was about the best captain I ever saw
in respect of placing his field. Brearley is also good at it. His
specialized knowledge has often stemmed the flow of runs.

Bowling a line and length are essential. The bad ball will be
punished at any level of cricket but in one-day cricket is much
more likely to be made to count. Line is important too because
a bowler can still bowl a good length and be slaughtered in one-
day matches if he is off the target. Batsmen take more risks and
get away with more in limited-overs games.

The bowler who drops it wide of the off stump, or outside leg,
can be hammered unmercifully. Of course, if it is too wide to
hit, then the umpires call a wide and the batting side has the
advantage of an extra delivery. To bowl wides or no-balls in
one-day cricket is a sin and no captain will happily tolerate it.

Jack Simmons, the Lancashire slow bowler who is known
around the circuit as 'Flat Jack', is one of the best bowlers in
one-day cricket because his length and line are always immacu-
late. They call him 'Flat Jack' because he doesn't give the ball
air, as he is prone to do in championship matches. He darts it
in, middle and leg, and defies the batsman to hit him. Right or
wrong, the county sides believe that one-day cricket is about
keeping the runs down and containing the opposition. Personally, I think they could attack more and try and bowl people
out and maintain attacking fields longer than they do.

The most commonly used tactic in one-day cricket is to bowl
at the stumps to a five–four field, five on the off and four on the
on side. Some bowlers, however, bowl off stump with a six–three
field but they run the risk of being lapped to leg.

The Gomes–Graham Barlow stand added 50 before both
batsmen were dismissed by Ratcliffe, a medium pacer who was
born in Accrington and who's been on the Lancashire staff
since 1971. After being released by Middlesex, Gomes joined
Learie Constantine's old club Nelson in the Lancashire League
and promptly beat Learie's batting record.

Phil Edmonds weighed in with some lusty fours against

Ratcliffe's bowling before being caught for 29, and Ratcliffe finished with 3–25 compared to Lee's 3–38 and Lever's 2–47. The last ten overs yielded 49. Barry Wood, 'Sticky' to his team mates, bowled twelve useful overs for 24 runs. He has been a fine one-day cricketer.

Though the light wasn't too good – they would probably have gone off in a Test match – the general view was that Lancashire would win to make it four triumphs in the Gillette Cup. But Lancashire failed to make a good start. Wood was bowled by Mike Selvey, and Frank Hayes was caught behind by John Murray off the bowling of Gomes. After thirty-eight overs, the score was only 73–2.

Clive Lloyd was blinking harder than usual behind his thick glasses when he came in at the fall of the second wicket. 'I can't see the ball,' he said. I must say he made a good fist of hitting it. He drove Fred Titmus straight at Mike Smith at mid on and Smith, normally such a reliable catcher, dropped it. That was the second crucial fielding mistake in the match and it was to prove costly because Lloyd, named Man of the Match by Tony Greig, went on to make 73 not out. He was soundly supported by the young left-hander Andrew Kennedy, who made 51 and later received the Cricket Writers' 'Young Cricketer of the Year' award. A promising future was forecast for Kennedy but in 1977 he lost his place in the side.

Brearley adopted the unusual practice of bowling Titmus and Selvey out, clearly banking on them to remove the top six in the Lancashire order. But Kennedy and Lloyd thwarted him, and Tim Lamb and Gomes had to be used when the pressure was on. Lancashire had three overs to spare when the winning run came. You need at least three seamers in one-day matches. That day Middlesex only had two, Selvey and Lamb, backed up by the medium pace of Gomes and the slow left-arm spin of Edmonds and the off-spin of Featherstone. A bowler of Wayne Daniel's pace would have made all the difference if he had been available at that time.

Lancashire were in the final again when I collected my next gold medal and £60 for standing in a Gillette Cup Final in

1976 and this time their opponents were Northamptonshire, who had never reached that far before. It was rightly described as one of the most entertaining finals of the competition. Northampton won by four wickets with eleven deliveries remaining, their first success in their ninety-eight-year history up to then.

Again, it was a dull, overcast day but there wasn't an excuse to put the other side in. David Lloyd won the toss and batted. There was a gasp right round the packed ground when John Dye, bowling from the Nursery end, bowled Farokh Engineer round his legs for a duck. *Wisden* described it as an inswinging yorker but I am afraid I have to correct them: it pitched on leg and took leg.

It might just have drifted down the hill a shade, that is all. But it certainly wasn't an inswinging yorker. Farokh said, 'You know, Dickie, I think I asked for the wrong guard.'

'What guard did you ask for?' I said. 'I asked for leg stump,' he said. 'But I gave you leg,' I said. He's mainly a legside player. In his anxiety to get the ball away through mid wicket, he went too far across his stumps.

Dye struck again when he got a ball to lift off a length and rap Barry Wood's fingers as he played back. Wood shook his hand and it was clear that he'd been seriously injured. He went off to hospital and an X-ray showed a broken bone. That was a bad blow for as well as needing his runs, Lancashire wanted his bowling. They were already missing Clive Lloyd, who was up at Scarborough with the West Indian touring side. Lloyd couldn't be released.

Frank Hayes went for 19 and Harry Pilling for 3 which left Lancashire 45–3, or four if you counted Wood. John Abrahams, born in South Africa, the son of Cecil Abrahams, the former Milnrow and Radcliffe professional in the Central Lancashire League, helped to add 95 for the 4th wicket with David Lloyd before Bishen Bedi came on to dismiss both of them in their forties.

Bedi wasn't used until the fortieth over. Up to then Mushtaq Mohammed had preferred Wayne Larkins and Peter Willey. But Bedi followed up by taking Bob Ratcliffe's wicket and

Mushtaq allowed him to bowl the last over of the innings to David Hughes though Dye and Alan Hodgson both had overs remaining.

Dye's figures were 7–3–9–1 and Hodgson's 6–3–10–1. It seemed rather odd that between them they should have eleven overs left while Larkins and Willey, neither of them front-line bowlers, should have bowled their quota.

Hughes smashed Bedi for 26 in that last over. It went 4, 6, 2, 2, 6, 6. And after each blow, Bedi politely applauded and said, 'Well hit.' Bishen is like that. He reckons he has a better chance of taking wickets if the batsman is trying to hit him. Johnny Wardle used to exploit flight the same way. He would hold the next ball up a little and often the batsman would be caught.

Only this time Hughes kept clearing the boundary. It was a repeat of his innings in the dark against Gloucestershire's John Mortimore in the same competition years earlier. Mortimore could have been faulted for his line but Bedi couldn't be criticized. Bedi bowled off and middle and Hughes kept pulling him out over mid wicket. The final flurry enabled Lancashire to reach 195–7, Hughes 39 not out, a defensible total.

With no Wood to bowl, Lancashire were reduced to three seam bowlers, Lever, Lee and Ratcliffe, with Simmons and Hughes as back up. Roy Virgin and Peter Willey, the Northampton openers, batted very sensibly with Willey particularly severe off the back foot. He is a good player and an unlucky one to have been discarded so soon by England. Perhaps if his chance had come earlier, he might have had a more successful international career.

Willey and Virgin put on 103 for the 1st wicket, Virgin 53 and Willey 65. When these two were out there seemed no danger of Northampton losing but, for some peculiar reason, the middle-order batsmen decided to hit out. David Steele had an uncharacteristic slog and he, Mushtaq, Larkins and Cook all went, and the tension returned.

Wicket keeper George Sharp calmed it down and with Sarfraz, no mean batsman, passed the target. Colin Cowdrey

gave the Man of the Match award to Willey. I spent an enjoyable half an hour or two having a glass of champagne with
Mushtaq and his players in their dressing-room. It is good for
cricket when the honours go round.

I have officiated in two Benson and Hedges Finals, Leicester
v. Surrey in 1974 and Kent *v.* Gloucestershire in 1977. Benson
Finals are much the same as Gillette Finals except the over limit
is fifty-five and not sixty. The tensions and pressures are the
same and the crowds make the same kind of noise.

The 1974 final was memorable for the first ever hat-trick in a
Benson Final. Ken Higgs, the former Lancashire and England
bowler since moved to Leicester, was the man who did it.
Higgs, whose England career had ended six years earlier and
who had retired before Mike Turner resurrected him, has
never been known as the most demonstrative of county
cricketers. If I remember, he didn't react in an over-excited
manner after Arnold Long was caught behind to follow Alan
Butcher and Pat Pocock back to the pavilion off successive balls.

His figures were remarkable: seven overs, two maidens, ten
runs, four wickets. Higgs isn't quick but when I played against
him I always jarred my hands as the ball struck the bat. As they
say in the trade, he hits the deck hard.

Surrey captain John Edrich was the anchorman in his side's
170 off 54.1 overs. After making only 18 from the first twenty-
four overs, he might have been caught and bowled by John
Steele, but Steele dropped it. That mistake cost Leicester 22
runs and they gave Surrey a further 30 runs when Robin
Jackman was missed.

But Steele was to catch and bowl Edrich for 40, the key
wicket. Freddie Brown, the adjudicator, made Edrich Man of
the Match, not Higgs, because of his captaincy as much as his
stalwart batting.

Leicester made a bad start and never recovered. Geoff
Arnold bowled Barry Dudleston with the first ball of the innings
and after a slow stand which took the total to 46 in nineteen
overs, both Mick Norman and Roger Tolchard were out lbw.
Steele was run out and the match was virtually over when

Edrich moved Geoff Howarth across into the covers, and next ball Brian Davison hit Arnold straight to him to provide a straightforward catch. Arnold (3–20), Roope (2–30) and Pat Pocock (3–26) all bowled economically but it was team work more than anything else that gained Surrey their first success in limited-overs cricket.

Whatever happens with the cigarette companies and advertising, the Benson and Hedges Cup is here to stay. Like the Gillette Cup, it is now a part of the cricketing calendar.

16
Soweto

Soweto is an African township outside Johannesburg, South Africa's largest city. It is the size of Manchester and stretches for miles and miles. Estimates of the population vary between 750,000 and 1,500,000 and, according to statistics, there are three sports stadia there, two swimming pools and eighty sports fields. But in most parts there is no power and light, no proper roads and no telephones.

Soweto breaks into the headlines when there are riots, which is often. The workers who live there get the trains in to Johannesburg every morning to work and they come back every night. I first went to South Africa to coach in 1965 but it was 1974 before I was invited into Soweto to coach. You need a permit to go there – and a police escort is also useful.

Friday is a bad day to go because the murder rate, consistently high, soars that day as workers come home with their wage packets. The most commonly used murder weapon is the bicycle spoke which is hidden up the sleeve. The assailant sticks it in the victim's chest, often piercing the heart and killing him. The killer steals the man's wage packet and makes off into the maze of unmade-up, dusty roads and little, two-room houses.

The cricket facilities in Soweto are extremely poor. There are no grass pitches of any note, only coconut mats stretched on grass in the middle of fields used normally for football. The first day I went there for coaching, no-one had arrived at the scheduled time of 9.30. I began to think I had come to the wrong field.

Then over the hill came a swarm of black youngsters. It was like a scene from the Michael Caine film *Zulu*. There were hundreds of them, perhaps thousands; it was impossible to count. Most of them had ragged, patched pants and wore no shoes. A few had sandals and one, I remember, wore a bowler and carried a brolly. None of them appeared to be dressed for cricket, nor did they seem to have any gear.

The man with the bowler said, 'Excuse me, are you Mr Dickie Bird, professor of cricket?' I said, 'That's me.' 'We're here for cricket coaching,' he said. 'Good,' I said, wondering how we were going to start. It was like sharing the five loaves and fishes out among the multitude.

I asked a group to mark out a pitch and they did so – but the stumps were sixty yards apart. They fished out a brand new cricket bag which contained some equipment from the sponsors. The balls were unused.

One youth started flicking the cricket ball up on his feet like a footballer. Then another one did it with a second ball. Soon they were playing soccer tricks with every available ball and I realized it was no use trying to show them how to play cricket: they were much happier playing football.

The Bantus of Soweto much prefer to play the fast, exciting sports. Cricket doesn't really suit their temperament. They like football, boxing and cycling in that order. Their footballing skills are immense and with training and the opportunity to develop, they could become a major force in world football.

They worship players like Pele, Eusebio and the great black players. When you mention the names of these famous sportsmen – and the names of cricketers like Gary Sobers and Clive Lloyd – their eyes light up. But Garrincha, Brazilian star of the 1958 and 1962 World Cups, is not quite as popular with them as he was before he went to Soweto on a visit. The blacks had heard so much about him that they were expecting something special. But Garrincha was well past his best and the locals said some of their players had more skill. They were probably right.

The Orlando Stadium in Soweto, which I went to, is a splendid stadium quite out of character with the place. The dressing-rooms, complete with tiled baths and showers, even have carpet on the floors. Attendances there are in the Manchester United class, up to 50,000 each match.

But the Bantu are not too well behaved as spectators. Regularly there are fights and riots at the stadium and the referee has to be a very brave man. Fireworks are continually going off and bottles are thrown indiscriminately. Several English officials, including the 1974 World Cup referee, Jack Taylor, have been attacked. Jack Taylor was struck by a bottle while refereeing the multi-racial final between Kaizer Chiefs, an all-black side, and Hellenic, an all-white side, at the Rand Stadium in Johannesburg in 1975 and the game was held up for twenty minutes while police calmed the rioters.

Sir Stanley Matthews has spent a considerable time coaching in Soweto under a scheme financed by Coca-Cola. Though in his sixties, he still plays football and trains daily. He is a fitness fanatic. On one visit to South Africa, I met him at a function paid for by Coca-Cola. We were lavishly entertained and it was a superb day out but Stan said he was going to ask for a fee for attending. I was quite put out that he should ask but that was his usual practice and he was sticking by it.

Willie Watson was there too. For some years Willie had been the ground manager at Wanderers Cricket Club in Johannesburg but had fallen out with someone and now worked for Fenners, the Hull-based company who made mining equipment for the gold mines, one of the biggest employers of black labour.

Though fifty-eight, Willie was still playing social cricket and enjoying it. We had a long chat recalling our times together at Yorkshire and Leicester. Another guest was Sid O'Linn, the former Kent cricketer and Charlton Athletic footballer, who now runs a big sports outfitting business in Johannesburg in partnership with Johnny Waite, the former Springbok wicket keeper, one of the finest ever Test keepers, who appeared in a record fifty Tests.

Sid was no friend of the umpire or referee in his playing days.

He was once sent off at Charlton and when he played cricket he never walked. 'The only time I walked, Dickie,' he said, 'was when I was going for a bus.' Sid was never capped by Kent and it still rankles with him.

The Bantus are not very interested in cricket but the Indians and Cape Coloureds are, and it was from the ranks of the Cape Coloureds that Basil D'Oliveira emerged. One or two other coloured cricketers from South Africa followed Dolly to England and played League cricket in the North but none have succeeded in emulating his progress into county and Test cricket. South Africa could have no finer ambassador to send here than Dolly. He has been a great servant to Worcester and English cricket and it is remarkable that he is still playing the first-class game at the age of forty-six.

The other end of the social scale from Soweto is St John's College, Johannesburg, the public school where I coached for a number of years. The boys used to arrive in chauffeur-driven Mercedes. Mercedes is the popular car in that part of South Africa. All my pupils were fully equipped, often with more than they needed.

On a trip to Rhodesia with a South African Under-15 side I met a boy named Williams who turned up with three brand new Gray-Nicholls bats specially imported from England. He scored three successive ducks, trying each of the bats in turn, and decided the bats weren't good enough so he gave them away! 'My mother will buy me some more,' he said.

There were six grass practice pitches at the school and a further six of batting laid on a sand base. They were all splendid batting pitches. In such conditions and in a climate ideally suited to the game, it was not surprising that the school produced some outstanding cricketers – Bruce Mitchell, who played forty-two Tests between 1929 and 1948, Russell Endean, twenty-eight Tests between 1951 and 1956 (now, incidentally, playing club cricket in London though in his mid-fifties) and the present Nottinghamshire captain Clive Rice.

The main school pitch is one of the finest in South Africa. It has both pace and bounce, features which are increasingly hard to find on many Test grounds nowadays, and is prepared by the traditional method of using plenty of water and liberal use of the heavy roller. The chief groundsman is a Zulu named Sithole and he has a team of lads under him who spend all their working hours on the square. Most of the time they sit there, picking out weeds and unruly bits of grass by hand.

Sithole told me once how much he was paid. It was a derisory amount. Even in England, groundsmen are not among the higher paid members of the cricketing fraternity.

Though the young white South African cricketer has these advantages, he works hard to make his way in the game. Most of them are dedicated but they know they stand little chance of becoming world-famous cricketers because South Africa is no longer a member of the International Cricket Conference and cannot take part in Test matches against another country.

I enjoyed my time in South Africa and wouldn't insult my many hosts there by trying to lecture them on their politics. The problem of South Africa is one that can only be solved from within by the people of South Africa themselves. It won't be easy. They've got to find a meeting place between the two extremes typified by Soweto and St John's College.

Progress is being made in multi-racial sport and there are now multi-racial leagues but it will be years before South Africa can get back into world cricket. By that time the great cricketers of recent times, Barry Richards, Graeme Pollock, Mike Procter and Eddie Barlow, will have stopped playing. They are the last Springboks who played Test cricket.

There is a promising new generation of batsmen but a deficiency in bowlers. One of the best young batsmen is Kepler Wessels, who played half a season for Sussex in 1977 before starting his National Service. He never hits the ball in the air and is a most disciplined player. Playing for Western Province, Eddie Barlow's side, is another excellent young batsman, Peter Kirsten.

Barlow still believes the South Africans could hold their own in a Test series against any of the major countries but I disagree. They have the batting, but not the bowling. These days the major wicket takers in Tests are fast bowlers and the Springboks don't have anyone in the class of Thomson, Lillee, Holding, Roberts or Willis.

Years of isolation have left them behind. Their fastest bowler is Garth Le Roux, who plays with Barlow at Western Province. Barlow rates him highly but in 1976, when I met him in England, he said to me, 'I didn't think human beings could bowl as fast as Holding, Roberts and Daniel.'

The South Africans used to have four world-class bowlers in the fifties in Peter Heine, Neil Adcock, Trevor Goddard and Hugh Tayfield but now they have only Procter. A bowler who would be effective in England, however, is the six-feet-six-inch tall Vincent van der Bijl of Natal. Van der Bijl has a big in-swinger and outswinger and with his height would be dangerous in English conditions. He regularly bowls more overs and takes more wickets than most other bowlers in the Currie Cup but lacks pace.

The only South African bowler signed by Kerry Packer was the leg-spinner and googly bowler Denys Hobson of Western Province. Hobson is like Chandrasekhar, the Indian bowler: he is quick through the air and makes it bounce. He, too, takes many wickets in South Africa and would be a success wherever he played. Two bowlers who play in English county cricket, Clive Rice (Nottinghamshire) and Paddy Clift (Leicestershire) are among the better bowlers in the Currie Cup. Rice is one of the outstanding all-rounders.

At the moment the black and coloured cricketers are nowhere near good enough to compete with these players. There are some Cape Coloureds who are nearly up to standard but it will take many more years before the blacks produce a Test-class player.

When Richie Benaud's Wanderers XI played a South African Invitation XI at Soweto in 1976 the Wanderers scored 331–7 with the Chappell brothers scoring half centuries and the South African XI could only muster 47. *Wisden* summed it up, 'The major interest of the tour came from the assessment of South African cricketing standards after the isolation from international cricket for six years.

'It was clear there were no fast bowlers or slow bowlers in the class of the best Australians but that South Africa possessed some effective fast medium bowlers. Richards and Pollock were in a class of their own though there were promising innings from Wessels, A. J. S. Smith and a more mature player, J. G. Heron.

'Of the eight players who were non-white used in the Invitation matches, only Ebrahim, slow left arm with Central Lancashire League experience, and Bergins, right arm fast medium, seemed at home in this company.'

I agreed with that assessment. Barry Richards, one of the greatest players the game has seen, has little incentive to keep reproducing his best. The young batsmen who follow him have even less.

During the Currie Cup Final between Transvaal and Western Province at the Wanderers ground, Johannesburg, in 1975, I was introduced to the South African Prime Minister, John Vorster. He doesn't say a lot but he knows sport, especially rugby. He seemed a down to earth, ordinary man with the South Africans' love of sport.

In a strong Afrikaans accent, he talked about the great cricketers he admired most, Barry Richards, Graeme Pollock and Mike Procter. We didn't discuss politics.

One of the tragedies of South Africa's isolation is that it prevents the top Test players from other countries playing on some of the world's finest cricket grounds. Newlands in Cape Town is one of the most picturesque cricket grounds in the world. It has Table Mountain in the background.

Wanderers in Johannesburg is South Africa's biggest ground, with a capacity of nearly 30,000. It is one of the largest sporting clubs, almost in the class of Real Madrid in Spain. The subscription is very expensive and membership is open only to white people. Kingsmead in Durban is a small ground near the sea, and the other Test ground is St George's in Port Elizabeth. The tour of South Africa used to be the most enjoyable for England cricketers. I love going back there.

17

Umpires

Overseas Test captains all agree that English umpires are the best in the world. One of the reasons why English umpires lead is that they are the only full-time professional umpires. In Australia, the West Indies, South Africa, Pakistan, India and New Zealand umpiring is a part-time occupation. Another advantage English umpires have is that they have all played first-class cricket, many of them at Test level. You could pick a useful side from any year's list of first-class umpires.

Perhaps the best known umpire in England was Frank Chester, who lost an arm in the First World War. Frank, who was born in 1896, was a very good batsman with Worcester, and a prolific scorer before his career was cut short. After one season on the list, he decided not to stand again but officials at Lord's persuaded him to change his mind. Quickly he became the outstanding umpire of his day. Some ex-players I have spoken to, men like Eric Rowan, Jack Cheetham, the former South African captain, and Johnny Waite, all agree that Chester was the top man in their time. Sir Don Bradman said the same thing.

Frank was a frequent user of malapropisms. Talking about a knee injury, he once said, 'I knew at once it was me cartridge.' The critic and broadcaster E. W. Swanton said of him, 'He was the most famous umpire of them all.'

Chester stood in forty-eight Tests, a record that will probably never be beaten. In his day, he stood in all five Tests in a series and the other umpires took turns to partner him. Today the maximum number of Tests each umpire is allowed in a series in England is generally two, but exceptions are made in the event of injury. I did three in 1973 and 1976 for that reason.

R. C. Robertson-Glasgow, one of the leading writers on cricket, once wrote of Chester, 'First-class umpiring is, as it should be, first class. But the standard is set from Chester. He stands for weeks without a mistake of sight or hearing. He changed umpiring from an occupation to an art. It was he who first bent low and balanced his face almost on the bails, and so began a fashion which reached far down into club cricket and only stopped short of these rural matches in which the bowler's umpire must stand erect to save his kidneys and balance the bails. Only an umpire as nearly infallible as Chester could afford to adorn so formal a task with powers of idiosyncrasy.'

Frank Chester suffered from ill health in his last years on the list. He was affected by ulcers when he handled the England *v.* Australia Test at Headingley in 1953 and Reg Simpson, the England opener, appeared to be two or three yards out of his ground when Frank gave him in. The Australians reacted in a manner which upset Chester. Next day he sent a telegram to Lord's saying he couldn't stand in the next match on his schedule. Two years later he retired and in 1957 he died.

The leading character umpire was undoubtedly Alec Skelding, the former Leicester pace bowler who was born in 1886 and died in 1960. Alec would always end the day's play by taking off the bails and saying, 'That, gentlemen, concludes the entertainment for the day.'

There are countless stories about him. In one match at Leicester he shouted from the middle to someone in the pavilion, 'Close that window. It's causing a draught out here.' In those days Grace Road was an open, windswept ground.

Alec wore spectacles and was always ribbed about his eyesight. Robertson-Glasgow said of him, 'To the batsman, he was a whizz of arms and a glint of spectacles.' Skelding wasn't a bad bowler, fastish often and infrequently fast. 'The spectacles,' he once said, 'are there for the look of the thing. I can't see without them and on hot days I can't see with them, as I'm bowling with steam in my eyes. So I do it on hearing only, and appeal twice an over.'

In 1948, he gave the Australian batsman Syd Barnes, another character, out lbw at Grace Road and Barnes was most upset about it. Back in the pavilion, Barnes asked him, 'How many pairs of specs do you have and where do you keep your blind dog?'

The two men met again in the Surrey v. Australians match at the Oval and in the meantime, Skelding wrote Barnes a note explaining that he had three pairs of spectacles, one for sixes, one for leg byes and one for lbw decisions. About the dog, he said he very much regretted that the animal wasn't allowed in at cricket grounds. There was a hilarious sequel because during the Oval match a dog ran out to the middle and Barnes swooped to pick it up. 'Here, Alec,' he said. 'I thought your dog never came to the ground.' The surprising fact about Alec's career was that he never stood in a Test match. Perhaps he was too much of a joker for the serious business of Test cricket!

Alec liked a drink. He was having a night out in a local pub one night when the landlord called time. Alec shook hands with everyone in the bar before going out through a door which led to a telephone booth. The others knew it was a telephone booth and he was the only one that didn't. A few seconds later he was back. 'I've inspected the light and it's unfit for play in there,' he said.

During his playing career he was playing in a match at Old Trafford against Lancashire and was given the task of looking after a member of the team who was notorious for his drinking habits. Alec took his charge out for a few drinks but the session went on and on and by the time the man was ready for bed, he was paralytic. Next morning, the man was still in a very bad way and when they staggered into the ground, Alec had to confess to the captain, 'Sorry, skipper, but he's in a terrible state. He won't be able to play.'

The captain was angry. 'He'll have to play,' he stormed. 'We've got no 12th man.' So they dressed the fellow and pushed

him out on to the field. There was a long discussion about where
to place him. 'Put him at fine leg,' said Skelding. 'I'll bowl off
stump and he won't have anything to do there.' The captain
agreed and the boozer went off down to fine leg.

First ball Alec bowled outside the off stump. Second ball, the
same. But third ball he let it slip down the legside and the
batsman glanced it fine towards the unsafe fielder. Skelding
shouted at him to meet it but the man missed the ball and ran
past it. As the crowd hooted with laughter, he turned and
described a full circle round the ball which had now come to
rest.

'Pick it up,' shouted Skelding. 'Let's have it here.' Eventually
the man located the ball, picked it up, and threw it into the
members' enclosure! Willie Watson once told me that Alec was
past it in his final years as an umpire but the captains always
voted for him to stay on because he was such a great character!

Dai Davies, who died at the age of seventy-nine in 1976, was a
respected Test umpire (twenty-three Tests in all). *Wisden* said
of him that 'he was always firm and decisive'. I had long chats
with Dai whenever I did games at Swansea, near his home.

He wouldn't let players argue. During the England *v.* South
Africa Test at the Oval in which he gave Eric Rowan out lbw
to Jim Laker, Rowan said, 'That was never out.' 'You look in
paper tomorrow morning,' said Dai.

One of the most revered umpires of post-war years was Sid
Buller, a Yorkshireman who died in 1970 while on duty in a
match at Edgbaston. I learned a lot from watching Sid. As a
player with Worcester – he was a good wicket keeper – he was
involved in a serious car crash while on the way to a match at
Chelmsford against Essex in 1939. Another player, Charlie
Bull, died in the crash.

Sid was appointed to the Test panel in 1959 and within a
year was in the middle of one of the game's biggest controversies.
It was blatantly obvious to everyone except the South Africans
that Geoff Griffin's action would never pass English umpires on
the 1960 tour. It wasn't Griffin's fault, but he had an action
which constantly infringed the laws.

In the Second Test at Lord's Frank Lee, Buller's colleague, no-balled Griffin eleven times for throwing and Griffin's career was effectively at an end. In the exhibition match that followed, because the Test finished early, Buller called Griffin four times in five balls from square leg and Griffin finished the over bowling under-arm, only to be called again by Lee because he hadn't notified the umpire that he was changing to under-arm! Griffin never played for South Africa again.

Quite unfairly, Sid was discriminated against by the South Africans, who objected to him standing again in the series. He didn't do another match in the Test series that summer but Lord's paid him as though he had been allowed to carry out his duties. Sid Buller was the first umpire to receive the MBE. He was also the first umpire to roll his sleeves up, a habit I admit I have copied because it suits me.

The late Paul Gibb was an interesting character among umpires. He lived in a caravan which he used to bring to matches. Paul was the biggest eater on the cricket circuit in his time, and he used to have bets on how many meals he could eat. Once on a tour in India, he consumed fourteen ice creams in succession. If anyone left food on his plate, he would eat it. He died in Guildford in 1977. He lived in a caravan and drove buses. An unusual man.

Another great character was Hugo Yarnold, the former Worcester wicket keeper and umpire who died in tragic circumstances in 1974. Hugo was a lovable little man, a former boxer and a pugnacious character. In one match, Worcester v. Gloucester, Hugo, who was keeping wicket, said to Sam Cook, who was batting, 'Give me your wicket and I'll give you mine when we bat.'

Cricketers sometimes did that in those days. Sam went forward, deliberately missed the ball and Hugo whipped the bails off. Later, when Hugo was batting, Sam said, 'Now come on, Hugo, give us your wicket.'

'Not likely,' said Hugo. 'It's your job to get me out.' I don't think Sam fell for that one again. Hugo entered the record books for his six stumpings and a catch, seven dismissals in all, against

Scotland at Broughty Ferry. *Wisden* recorded the event but
missed out part of the story. When Hugo needed one more
stumping, he said to the Scotland tailender who had just come
in, 'Young lad, the only way to play this fellow is to go down the
pitch and hit him out of sight.' The batsman thought Hugo
was trying to be helpful to a young player. The batsman
charged forward to Roley Jenkins' leg-break, missed, and Hugo
stumped him. 'Bad luck, lad,' said Hugo. He got many of his
victims off the unorthodox bowling of Roley Jenkins. It wasn't
easy to take.

In his last four years as a player, Hugo had both kneecaps
removed but battled on. As an umpire, he was a conscientious,
respected figure and he stood in three Tests in 1967 and 1968.
Towards the end, his breathing was badly affected and sometimes he could barely draw breath. I used to say to him, 'Why
don't you give up smoking?' He was a heavy smoker. 'Nay, lad,'
he would say. 'You've got to have a cig.'

Sam Cook stood with him in his last match, Northampton *v.*
Essex at Wellingborough. Hugo was obviously very unwell but
turned down Sam's offer to drive him to his Worcester home.
An hour or two later, Hugo died when his car ran into an eight-
wheel lorry at Leamington. He was fifty-seven.

A cricketer who was very hostile to umpires in his playing
days became a good umpire himself – George Pope of Derby. I
never thought he would join the ranks of umpires, but he did. I
played against George in the Yorshire League in his final years
as a player. He was a big inswing bowler and also bowled leg
cutters. He was always appealing for lbw, most times when he
knew the ball was going down the legside.

He acted like a real pro with the less experienced umpires in
the League. He would appeal and on being told 'Not out' would
say, 'Good decision, sir.' After another appeal for a delivery
which was clearly missing, he said, 'Aye, that were close. Just
missing.' By this time the umpire would be feeling sympathetic.
Finally, he would let out an almighty appeal. 'How about that
then?' and more times than not, the umpire would raise the
finger.

Ron Lay, an umpire who has now retired, was one of the few people to make me upset on a cricket field. We were playing at Stroud and just before the close, the sky was so black that most cars in the road outside had their headlights on. I kept saying to him, 'What about the light?' but he said, 'Play on, it's all right.' I somehow survived until the last over but was out on the fifth ball of the last over. That really made me angry! I gave him the nickname 'O-lay' the Bandit. He had a Mexican-type moustache and dark hair and a habit of whipping his hand up quickly, just like a bandit making a fast draw, to give batsmen out. I wasn't happy with him then but I had many laughs with him subsequently.

Ray Illingworth has suggested that Lord's should start a coaching scheme for umpires to increase the flow of recruits and raise standards. But this is one area where I disagree with Ray. I think the standard is high enough. You can't coach umpires. Umpires are born, not made. You can learn the laws backwards and forwards and every way there is but that isn't the secret of successful umpiring.

Knowing the laws is only a small part. The real job is standing up to the pressure and commanding the respect of the players. No-one can be taught that. It is a natural gift. It is significant that nearly all the top umpires were players one year and umpires the next, without taking a course. The transition is simple, if you have the right qualities.

18

The Future

No-one will ever convince me that professional cricket is a bad life. It is comparatively well paid, enjoyable to take part in and you don't have to get up early in the morning. It is not like having to get up at 4.30 a.m. to go down the mine. You don't get dirty like steel workers, dustmen, firemen, car mechanics and factory workers. It is a healthy open-air life with a lot of prestige and glamour attached to it.

Yet in the past year or two there has been a tremendous up-heaval over the question of whether the players are paid enough. More money has come into cricket and players have started to compare themselves with performers in other sports. It has led to the Kerry Packer invasion and caused the biggest-ever threat to the future of the established game. I am all in favour of people making as much money as they can from their employers – though that doesn't necessarily bring with it happiness – but in any business you can't take out more than is paid in.

There is no profit to be made in running county cricket clubs. There are no shareholders and the people who control them, the members of the committees, are not paid and receive no dividends. Until a few years ago, the prospects for several of the counties were extremely bleak. Attendances at three-day matches were so low that often receipts failed to cover expenses.

The introduction of one-day competitions and the increased commercialization of Test matches have largely removed the danger of some of the counties going out of existence. Sponsorship has brought in large amounts of money and it is natural that the players expect to be paid a bigger share of the available cash.

The plight of the cricketer, if you could call it that, has been compared to the riches of the successful tennis players and the top golfers. But I think it is unrealistic to compare, say, Bob Willis with Jimmy Connors. Bob Willis is taking part in a team game whereas Jimmy Connors is on his own. Similarly with the golfers. Golf is an individual game. Not many golfers earn the same money as Johnny Miller or Jack Nicklaus. Often those at the other end of the scale are very poorly paid in comparison.

I agree that the players should earn more in cricket if they are helping to make the game a more viable enterprise. That makes sense. But a percentage of the takings has to be retained to keep the structure of county cricket in being. Without county cricket, which is still poorly attended in many parts of the country, there would be no arena for cricketers to learn to become Test-class cricketers.

County cricket, one hundred years old in 1977, should be here for a long time to come. It will never be well attended, not so long as people have to work during the week. But the interest in the traditional rivalries between counties will remain. Millions of people will still turn to their sports pages to find out who scored what and who took the wickets.

People are always coming up with ideas to improve county cricket. One of the most popular ideas is to play matches over four days instead of three. I don't agree with that myself. If the weather is fine, there is no reason why a two-innings match ought not to end in three days.

If there were lots of ex-county cricketers now on the dole or in poor circumstances, I could understand the arguments of those who say the current players are underpaid. I cannot think of one player I met in my career who is now down on his uppers. But I can think of hundreds who are successful businessmen.

Cricket may be a short life but it enables you to meet business people and make valuable contacts. The glamour attached to it means that it can be easier to get a job than it is for the ordinary man.

Of the Yorkshire side I played with in the fifties, none, to my
knowledge, is a poor man today. Doug Padgett is a coach with
Yorkshire and Don Wilson is the coach of the Indoor School at
Lord's, both reasonably well paid, secure jobs. Bryan Stott runs
his own plumbing business. Ronnie Burnett is in insurance. Vic
Wilson owns his own farm. Ken Taylor is a school teacher.
Jimmy Binks works for Fenners of Hull and Willie Watson
works for the same firm in South Africa.

Bob Platt owns an electrical shop. Mel Ryan owns news-
agents shops in Huddersfield. Johnny Wardle owns a country
club. Billy Sutcliffe has a sports outfitters in Leeds and Brian
Close has just retired from county cricket with a £35,000 tax-
free benefit. Jack Birkenshaw and Ray Illingworth are still
playing and Illingworth has a confirmed job as Yorkshire
manager when he quits Leicester. And as for Fred Trueman,
he will not be short of brass. He does a Sunday newspaper
column, appears on radio and TV and worked in 1977–8 as a
commentator for Kerry Packer in Australia. All of these players
became successful in their cricketing after-life. And I do not
think Yorkshire is untypical. A similar story could be repeated
at other counties.

Traditional cricket will survive because it has been proved
there is a market for it. The crowds for the Australia v. India
series compared favourably with attendances at Packer matches
even though it was virtually an Australian second eleven. And
the cricket was infinitely more interesting.

With the World Series Cricket run by the Packer organization, it was impossible to keep up with who was playing whom.
The matches seemed meaningless. There wasn't the thrill of
country playing country. It was one lot of Packermen playing
another lot of Packermen.

Just as in the 1970 Rest of the World series in England, the
public did not support the matches as well as they did traditional
Test matches. Packer countered this by saying he was more interested in the TV ratings than attendances. From a TV angle,
he said, the matches were a great success.

But I wonder whether the players, deep down, would agree

with that. I remember once watching Shirley Bassey in a concert at Liverpool and the theatre was nearly empty. I wondered what effect that had on Miss Bassey, and how it affected her performance.

I am convinced that performers don't perform as well in front of small audiences. Comedians and singers need a big audience to stimulate them and so do professional cricketers. I know I feel more excited when I go out to a big crowd in a Test at Lord's than I do if it is a nearly empty county ground.

When Australia last met the West Indies Down Under in an official series, attendances at the Melbourne ground twice exceeded 90,000. Yet when Australian and West Indian elevens met in World Series matches, there were less than a tenth of that number of spectators present. I think the Australian public demonstrated whose side it was on in cricket's battle and the authorities should be reassured by that verdict.

There could be room for a circus-type organization to promote its matches in conjunction with official matches but personally I doubt it. You cannot serve two masters. A footballer playing for Arsenal can't play for Tottenham Hotspur the next week, a Manchester United player can't turn out for Manchester City. The players will have to decide which side they will want to be on.

Whatever happens with Packer cricket, I feel traditional cricket will survive and continue to prosper. Probably more sponsorship will be attracted into the game as advertisers realize its potential.

One advantage of the Packer business is that it is bringing to the fore new and exciting talent, players who would not otherwise have the chance of playing Test cricket. The Pakistan side has benefited in this respect and so has the Australian team. Test players only become Test players by playing in Test matches. If they don't get the opportunity, they will never make Test players.

Paul Downton, the Kent wicket keeper, would probably never have been picked for England's last tour of Pakistan but for Packer. Nor would Phil Edmonds. Even without these changes, I believe the future of English cricket is very rosy. There are many good young players coming into the game, especially batsmen.

The 1975 World Cup rekindled interest in the game and the momentum was maintained in the following two years as cricket re-established itself as the national sport. I have seen this myself at the lower levels of the game. I have been helping Mike Fearnley, the Yorkshire coach, coaching boys in the winter at the Headingley nets. Never have I seen such a wealth of talent. One youngster, Tim Boon, aged fifteen, reminds me of Brian Close when he started at the same age. Boys of that age can sometimes fail to progress but this lad looks as though he could go to the top.

Around the counties, there is a profusion of talented players, among them David Smith, the twenty-two-year-old Warwickshire opener, son of Ken Smith, the former Northumberland and Leicester player, Chris Tavare of Kent, David Gower of Leicester, David Rock of Hampshire, Kevin Sharp of Yorkshire and two more young wicket keepers who will rival Downton for the right to succeed Alan Knott – Andy Brassington of Gloucester and Jack Richards of Surrey. I have been very impressed by all these players.

Abroad, Bobby Simpson would never have made a comeback but for Packer. I felt at the time that Simpson still had many years of Test cricket left when he retired in the late sixties. His re-emergence has been another plus from recent events in world cricket.

Like the players, umpires have had their salaries increased since the upheavals began. Many umpires do other jobs in the winter but it is not easy to find employment for six months only in a year.

The idea of having a couple of overseas umpires in the English county season has been shown to be a good one and it has been followed by the notion that there should be neutral umpires in Tests. I would love to umpire Australia *v.* West Indies in Australia, or West Indies *v.* Pakistan in the West Indies, but I cannot imagine the local umpires would be too keen on the idea – it would reduce their chances of standing in Tests! Similarly, English umpires wouldn't like foreign umpires standing in Test matches here. But a system of inter-changing umpires could possibly be worked out to everyone's advantage so that Tests would have one local and one foreign umpire officiating. The expense would not be too great.

I have enjoyed my years as a first-class umpire and hope there will be many more to come. Cricket is the finest game there is and I love being part of it. I trust my white cap will be around for some years yet and that I won't need a white stick to go with it.